Liz Winfeld

Straight Talk About Gays in the Workplace
Creating an Inclusive, Productive Environment for Everyone in Your Organization
Third Edition

D0165352

Straight Talk About Gays in the Workplace

Creating an Inclusive, Productive Environment for Everyone in Your Organization

Third Edition

HAWORTH Gay & Lesbian Studies
John P. De Cecco, PhD
Editor in Chief

The Man Who Was a Woman and Other Queer Tales from Hindu Lore by Devdutt Pattanaik

How Homophobia Hurts Children: Nurturing Diversity at Home, at School, and in the Community by Jean M. Baker

The Harvey Milk Institute Guide to Lesbian, Gay, Bisexual, Transgender, and Queer Internet Research edited by Alan Ellis, Liz Highleyman, Kevin Schaub, and Melissa White

Stories of Gay and Lesbian Immigration: Together Forever? by John Hart

From Drags to Riches: The Untold Story of Charles Pierce by John Wallraff

Lytton Strachey and the Search for Modern Sexual Identity: The Last Eminent Victorian by Julie Anne Taddeo

Before Stonewall: Activists for Gay and Lesbian Rights in Historical Context edited by Vern L. Bullough

Sons Talk About Their Gay Fathers: Life Curves by Andrew R. Gottlieb

Restoried Selves: Autobiographies of Queer Asian/Pacific American Activists edited by Kevin K. Kumashiro

Queer Crips: Disabled Gay Men and Their Stories by Bob Guter and John R. Killacky

Dirty Young Men and Other Gay Stories by Joseph Itiel

Queering Creole Spiritual Traditions: Lesbian, Gay, Bisexual, and Transgender Participation in African-Inspired Traditions in the Americas by Randy P. Conner with David Hatfield Sparks

How It Feels to Have a Gay or Lesbian Parent: A Book by Kids for Kids of All Ages by Judith E. Snow

Getting It On Online: Cyberspace, Gay Male Sexuality, and Embodied Identity by John Edward Campbell

Pederasts and Others: Urban Culture and Sexual Identity in Nineteenth-Century Paris by William A. Peniston

Men, Homosexuality, and the Gods: An Exploration into the Religious Significance of Male Homosexuality in World Perspective by Ronald E. Long

Mucho Macho: Seduction, Desire, and the Homoerotic Lives of Latin Men by Chris Girman

Side by Side: On Having a Gay or Lesbian Sibling edited by Andrew R. Gottlieb

Gay Catholic Priests and Clerical Sexual Misconduct: Breaking the Silence edited by Donald L. Boisvert and Robert E. Goss

Straight Talk About Gays in the Workplace: Creating an Inclusive, Productive Environment for Everyone in Your Organization, Third Edition by Liz Winfeld

Straight Talk About Gays in the Workplace
Creating an Inclusive, Productive Environment for Everyone in Your Organization

Third Edition

Liz Winfeld

HPP

Harrington Park Press®
An Imprint of The Haworth Press, Inc.
New York • London • Oxford

For more information on this book or to order, visit
http://www.haworthpress.com/store/product.asp?sku=5403

or call 1-800-HAWORTH (800-429-6784) in the United States and Canada
or (607) 722-5857 outside the United States and Canada

or contact orders@HaworthPress.com

Published by

Harrington Park Press®, an imprint of The Haworth Press, Inc., 10 Alice Street, Binghamton, NY 13904-1580.

First edition published by the American Management Association, 1995. Second edition published by The Haworth Press, 2001, © Liz Winfeld and Susan Spielman.

Cover design by Kerry E. Mack.

Library of Congress Cataloging-in-Publication Data

Winfeld, Liz.
    Straight talk about gays in the workplace : creating an inclusive, productive environment for everyone in your organization / Liz Winfeld.—3rd ed.
        p.   cm.
    Includes bibliographical references and index.
    ISBN 1-56023-546-2 (hard : alk. paper) — ISBN 1-56023-547-0 (soft : alk. paper)
    1. Homosexuality in the workplace. 2. Gays—Employment. 3. Lesbians—Employment. 4. Diversity in the workplace. 5. Employee fringe benefits. 6. Sexual orientation. I. Title.

HD6285.W56 2005
658.3'0086'64—dc22
                                                                        2004027752

This third edition of "Straight Talk . . ." is dedicated to the literally dozens of diversity champions I've met over the past twelve years who have put themselves on the line standing up for what they believe in. These people are gay, lesbian, bisexual, transgender, and straight. They are HR professionals, executives, and just employees in any number of positions who simply chose to stand up for principles of inclusion and equality—often at great personal risk to their reputations or to their very livelihoods. I cannot list you all, but I have met you all, and you know who you are. I am honored to know you and humbled by your courage. Your integrity is awe-inspiring and my respect for you all is boundless. I can do the work that I do only because of you, and I never forget it.

And to my mom and dad—Bev and Sid—you are my heroes. Keep spending my inheritance no matter how much I complain about it.

ABOUT THE AUTHOR

Liz Winfeld holds an MA in Education and is the President of Common Ground, an education/consulting firm specializing in workplace diversity beyond race and gender. She is a nationally recognized expert in workplace diversity specific to sexual orientation, gender identity, and domestic partner benefits. Liz co-authored the first two editions of *Straight Talk About Gays in the Workplace,* the first edition of which became a National Library Award winner. She is also author/editor of *A Trainer's Guide to Training Tough Topics,* is co-author of *The Web Conferencing Book,* and has authored several articles. Through the years, she has been a speaker for The Conference Board, the AMA, SHRM, ASTD, *Working Women Magazine,* Bennett College, Duke University, Work Worlds, and the Minnesota Work Worlds Alliance. Her work has also appeared in the *Washington Post, Reuters, Bloomberg Business Network,* the *Wall Street Journal,* the Associated Press, the *Boston Globe, USA Today,* and several other major publications.

Common Ground's clients include MasterCard International, the NSA, Hasbro Corporation, Deluxe Financial Services, Hewlett-Packard, Quest Diagnostics, American Express, Ford Motor Company, The Prudential, Nike, Aetna, Kaiser Permanente, McDonald's Corporation, Classic BMW, State Farm, NOAA, Shell Oil, Motorola, JP Morgan/Chase, Best Buy Corporation, Caribou Coffee, and Honda of America to name just a few.

CONTENTS

Chapter 1

The Changing Landscape

A great deal has changed since the first edition of *Straight Talk About Gays in the Workplace: Creating an Inclusive, Productive Environment for Everyone in Your Organization.* The author credit has changed as I have written this edition on my own. If you learn nothing else from this book, learn this: writing a book is a great deal like what I understand giving birth to a child is like. I am not the biological parent of a child so I can only go by what my friends who are biological mothers tell me—if you go through labor once, you won't want to do it again. Writing a book is a similarly intense process that I swore I'd never do again . . . and here I am, on number three. (Several of my friends have more than one kid, too, by the way.)

Perhaps most significantly, I have changed. Some of these changes are due in no small part to a couple of curveballs that life has tossed me in the past decade, but that hardly makes me unusual. I'm not the only one who's had ample opportunity to practice making lemonade out of lemons. It's a common human desire—or necessity—to make the best of bad situations. Sexual orientation and gender identity are also common to all humans. We all have a sexual orientation and we all have a gender identity. It's a common ground we can build on, and for ten years, that's what I've been trying to do.

Beyond the changes I've experienced as an individual on the planet, the changes that most affect my work as an educator and consultant in workplace diversity are entirely external. I'm referring to the progression of human knowledge and resulting attitudes about orientation and identity that are occurring worldwide and almost daily. And, most important, they are the changes I've experienced because of the people I've met and worked with. I thought running Common Ground was going to be only a job. It turned out to be one hell of an interesting adventure.

DEALING WITH WHAT IS NOW

This book is more than just the third edition; it's the next iteration of our collective growth around these topics, and it's certainly the next step on my personal journey to better understand—and better explain—the salient issues of sexual orientation and gender identity in the workplace.

For instance, there was so much to discuss about sexual orientation when we wrote the first and second editions that it didn't even occur to us to include a discussion of gender identity, or what are commonly called transgender issues. Excluding them then was made simpler by the fact that, in 1994 and even 1998, the common misconception was that there were no transgender people in our workplaces. In 1994, lesbian and gay people had just started to pop up on workplace radar screens, it having been widely assumed until at least 1992, when Lotus became the first publicly traded company to offer same-sex domestic partner benefits, that all gay people worked for Levi Strauss & Co. in San Francisco, with a few gays and lesbians having managed to sneak into AT&T (but only in the Northeast), IBM, Apple, and Microsoft.

When I first started Common Ground, only six states had nondiscrimination laws pertaining in any way to employment rights that included sexual orientation; none of them included gender identity. As of March 1, 2004, fourteen states have laws inclusive of sexual orientation and pertaining to employment, among other things, and four of them specifically include transgender people. Eight states in ten years might seem rather slow, but it's better than nothing, and the truth is that changes are coming more rapidly now.

So to begin, I think it's prudent to take a look at where we, as a society, are in our opinions about parts of life that are intrinsically entwined with sexual orientation and gender identity, because no positive work can ever be done on human diversity in the workplace unless we strive to meet people where they are. I acknowledge that I would like people to be further along, that I sometimes wish I could flick a switch and have people get it. But I also know that almost nothing worth doing is ever easy, and so I continue to try to build public awareness and knowledge, brick by brick.

It comes as no surprise to anyone who's paying attention, even a little, to the world going by these days that issues of sexual orientation and gender identity are reaching a fever pitch in terms of the speed and number at which they are introduced into the broader culture. It would be difficult to find a person, regardless of orientation, who is not aware that the times are a-changin' relative to these things, and I believe that people want to participate in the discussions about them in meaningful ways. In order to do that, they have to know what they're talking about, and that's where this book and diversity education about sexual orientation and gender identity play a major role.

IT'S ABOUT ALL PEOPLE

Before I get to the ways in which our world is changing around these aspects of human diversity, it's important for us all to realize that when we are talking about sexual orientation we are talking about everyone. Therefore, laws or policies or programs that pertain to sexual orientation pertain to all people. If it's illegal for an employer in a given jurisdiction to discriminate against someone on the basis of real or perceived sexual orientation, then heterosexual as well as homosexual people are protected by that law. The fact that people don't seem to get that, or sometimes claim not to in order to push their own political and social agendas, is a major problem in moving these issues forward in the workplace and in society. For the same reason that we have affirmative action or EEO (Equal Employment Opportunity) laws, Title VII of the 1964 Civil Rights Act, or suspect classes in the U.S. Constitution, we also must have protections for people on the basis of sexual orientation. The truth is that we don't live in a perfect world where everyone lets everyone be who they are or who they say they are. We live in a world where protections are necessary for some groups of people for a period of time or, maybe it will turn out, forever. It's not "special rights" for gay people, as some of the more hysterical, divisive members of the religious right scream (repeatedly and without anything resembling rationality). It's about equal rights and protections for all people based on real or perceived sexual orientation and gender identity.

Here's an example. About five years ago, a young man who is straight walked into a gay bar in Provincetown, Massachusetts, the home of many gay bars, and asked for a summer job. He was told that the bar "didn't hire straight boys," and he sued them for employment discrimination on the basis of sexual orientation. He won his suit because such discrimination is illegal in Massachusetts and in thirteen other states.

It must be understood from the start that "sexual orientation" is not "code" for "homosexuality" or for "gay issues." Sexual orientation is an inherent characteristic of all people. We are, each of us, heterosexual, homosexual, bisexual, or asexual. I understand that most people don't understand what these words mean, but that's why you'll find very good explanations of them all in this book and that's why I do the work I do. Give me two or three hours with a bunch of folks and they will still have questions or different opinions about things related to sexual orientation, but they will also know precisely what it is they are talking or thinking about. From there, let the discussions begin.

THE INHERENT ARGUMENT

I find it amazing, and vaguely un-American, for people to insist that the civil rights of other human beings in this country should be determined by popular vote, or that when judges make decisions such as the one that found sodomy laws to be unconstitutional or those allowing same-sex civil marriage, they are called "liberal activist judges." Some people have a short memory. For instance, if it were still left to popular vote or not acted upon by the judiciary, in many parts of this country women would likely still not have the right to vote, interracial marriage would still be illegal, and segregation would still be the law. Indeed, in countries governed more by religious doctrine and less by rule of law or common sense, women can't vote and minorities are still enslaved. Winning civil rights is always a messy, complicated battle, and all avenues must be leveraged by people on the different sides of any issue. That is the American way, and it's fair because it's available to all. There's a reason why there are three branches of government. This was good thinking on the part of the founding fathers. The people who complain about activist judges don't seem to have too much of a problem when other judges rule it's okay to post the Ten Commandments in public buildings, despite the protests of many based on a fervent belief in the separation of church and state, or who force upon women a restrictive view of their right to have a safe abortion.

Speaking of the founding fathers, one has to conclude that statistically, based on knowledge of human sexuality, at least 10 percent of them were either gay or bisexual. I have a theory that if even a couple of them had admitted as much back at the original Constitutional Convention then perhaps they would have made provisions for people who were other than heterosexual. Of course, this theory is full of holes because they obviously knew that there were black people and women all over the place and hardly any provisions were made for them. Black men were counted as three-fifths of a person, and women, regardless of color, weren't counted for anything at all. Their unusual lack of foresight in some matters has necessitated changes such as the Bill of Rights, civil rights acts, and constitutional amendments to fill in some particularly gaping holes. So, why don't people on the religious right complain about the "special rights" granted to them in the Bill of Rights (freedom of or freedom from religion) or in Title VII of the 1964 Civil Rights Act, which guarantees that a person's religious convictions are respected no matter what? Why don't people complain that EEO statutes extended to race, religion, national origin, color, or sex are special rights and are also double-dipping for some because they're also covered by the classification of "suspect classes" in the Constitution? Why? Because it wouldn't serve their purpose of demonizing gay, lesbian, bisexual, and transgender people, that's why. Or they'll say that a person doesn't choose his or her race or sex or national origin or religion. Or do they?

Think about this: I believe that a person's religious affiliation and moral code of conduct are more a matter of choice than sexual orientation is. I believe that orientation is absolutely inherent in humans and in any animal that sexually reproduces, and I believe that the data substantiate this.

For instance, on March 9, 2004, Reuters reported that U.S. researchers at the Oregon Health and Science University School of Medicine found certain groups of brain cells that were different in the parts of brains in rams and ewes that control sexual behavior.[1] Animal experts have found that about 8 percent of domestic rams display preferences for other males as sexual partners. These differences are documented not only in the construct of the brains of homosexual versus heterosexual animals but also in their hormonal constructs.[2]

In *Biological Exuberance: Animal Homosexuality and Natural Diversity* (1998),[3] Bruce Bagemihl documents homosexuality in more than 450 species of sexually reproducing animals and plants that he chose to study.

One could certainly ask, "who cares?" and in all honesty, that question occurs to me quite regularly. When people fully incorporate their sexual orientation in their lives, it takes on a meaning that can be described only as trivial. If I were to ask 100 heterosexual people what they thought about being heterosexual, more than ninety-five of them would tell me that they give it little or no thought at all. I know this because I've done it.

On the flip side, ask 100 fully incorporated gay people what they think of their sexual orientation and they too will say that they don't think about it much. Again, I know this because I've done it.

But the truth is, for better or for worse, people do care about the origins of sexual orientation, and it does seem to matter to some whether a person's orientation is determined by nature or nurture or choice. In declaring, with no doubt at all, that I believe orientation, like race, handedness, eye color, skin color, hair composition, and so on, is absolutely hardwired in the genetic makeup of a given individual, I have to face two matters that are also very certain. First, nothing about humanity or nature is that simple; and second, if there is a genetic disposition of human sexual orientation, then some extremely disturbed people will try to find it and eradicate it as if it were a disease.

Science has been looking for a "gay gene" for a long time. Absent a genetic connection to sexual orientation, scientists and sociologists have similarly been seeking an explanation for why some people are straight and why some are gay.

The most famous study having to do with sexual orientation was done by Alfred Kinsey, as presented in two books: *Sexual Behavior in the Human Male* (1948) and *Sexual Behavior in the Human Female* (1953).[4] Whereas many people purport that Kinsey found that 10 percent of people are homosexual (or words to that effect), he stated no such thing. Rather, Kinsey created a scale of human sexual response from 0 to 6, zero denoting exclusive heterosexuality and six denoting exclusive homosexuality. Just the fact that he created a scale should tell us all something.

Kinsey believed that human sexual orientation, a term he didn't have at his disposal at the time, was determined by three factors: predisposition to a certain sexual trigger, behavior, and thoughts/fantasies. Based on these three factors and surveys of first 6,000 men and then 6,000 women for his reports, Kinsey came to many conclusions. Among these he found that upwards of 37 percent of the male population had engaged in a homosexual experience after adolescence, 13 percent had been primarily homosexual since then, and 4 percent had been exclusively homosexual since then. For women, 13 percent had a homosexual experience since adolescence, 7 to 10 percent had been primarily homosexual since then, and 2 percent had been exclusively homosexual since then.

Since Kinsey's study, the percentages reported for homosexuality in the human animal have been as low as 2 percent and as high as 15 percent. Studies that also attempt to include bisexuality have gone as high as 20 percent. Obviously, no one has found a way to answer this question to everyone's satisfaction. But the question I have is, even if it were only 1 percent of all humanity since the beginning of time, what would it matter? Does might make right? Do sheer numbers decide what is equitable, just, moral? I just don't think so.

Scientists Dean Hamer and Simon LeVay have done research on the genetic predisposition to sexual orientation, that is, whether someone will experience a human sexual response in reaction to stimulus from a person of the same sex, the opposite sex, or both sexes. A study of female twins in 1993 found that almost 50 percent of identical twin sisters of gay women were gay themselves. Another study, released in July 1993, reported a link of male homosexuality to an area on the X chromosome. Hamer also released, in July 1993, a study that found more than 75 percent of a group of pairs of gay brothers had inherited identical DNA markers on a particular region of the X chromosome, which indicates a hereditary predisposition.[5]

None of this constitutes finding a gay gene, but it remains unclear whether such evidence is warranted, necessary, or even remotely useful. There currently is no finding of a handedness gene or of a gene for eye color, intelligence, cancer, height, baldness, athletic ability, skin tone, muscle mass, resistance or susceptibility to viruses, Tay-Sachs, or many other human characteristics. Yet these we accept as being inherent to the person and attribute them in part to heredity (baldness, height, susceptibility) and in part to practicing and building upon whatever it is you are equipped with (athletic ability, intelligence).

WHAT DO WE REALLY CHOOSE?

Although you may be born into a family unit that is Catholic or Jewish or Buddhist or any one of the other 9,000 or more religions on the planet, you still have to learn its teachings and, if you choose, you can agree or disagree with them. You can accept them or reject them. You can decide to continue being Jewish or not. But ask yourself this, if you happen to be heterosexual: Can you decide to stop being heterosexual? Sure, you can act as though you are homosexual if you want to. You can find someone of the same sex who agrees to help you adopt the role of a gay person. You can buy a house with this person, have sex, adopt kids, and do anything gay people do. But just because you are *acting* gay would not mean that you *are* gay. You'd still be straight; you can choose to act however you'd like.

Some people who insist that gays are looking for "special rights based on a choice of lifestyle" can point to questionable interpretations of parts of the Bible. They are entitled to their interpretation of that book, or this one, or any other for that matter, but it's still only an interpretation. It's not an absolute. There are no absolutes. That is entirely the point. One person's civil and human rights cannot—and must not—be at the discretion of other people based on a religious interpretation that serves some political or social agenda of moral superiority.

Some people are straight, some are gay, some are bisexual, some are asexual, and some are transgender. Furthermore, people of all orientations have different points of view when it comes to their understanding of orientation or their religious affiliations. Some are deeply religious (whatever that means), some are casually religious (whatever that means), and some are not religious at all. No one of us, regardless of where we fall on any one of these scales, is superior to anyone else, and while I will support a person's right to have whatever opinion she or he wants, I will not agree that this opinion—be it based on religious convictions or anything else—trumps my civil and human rights.

I've come to appreciate a basic fact about the work that I do. If I walk into a room of 100 people who've come to hear me speak about sexual orientation or gender identity in the workplace or in society, I know that 10 percent of them are so far to the right in terms of their religious and political convictions that they won't hear a thing I say no matter what I say. But I also know that 10 percent are so far to the left that they won't hear me either. The people on the right would describe themselves (and I'd describe them) as being ultra-conservative in their political and social thinking and absolutely fundamentalist in their interpretation of whatever scripture it is that they adhere to.

The people on the left, on the other hand, tell me that I am not "queer enough" for them. I am not in people's faces enough; I am too mainstream; I am not radical enough in my opinions or appearance. They happen to be absolutely right; I am not queer at all and I don't like being called queer. It's a silly word that, when trying to encompass so many different types of people within the realms of sexual orientation and gender identity, ends up meaning nothing at all.

The rest of the people in the room, the vast majority who are young, old, white, black, gay, straight, Democrat, Republican, liberal, or conservative, are just like me. I try to direct my comments to them because I know that they have honest questions, concerns, or opinions that are not based on the somewhat pointless rhetoric of either the left or the right. They're just regular people. They're the people who have always been responsible for change since the world began. There's no doubt that radical thinking on one side or the other has always spurred the action, but when all is said and done, it's when the rather average majority gets involved that things begin to move in any meaningful way either to the left or the right or, in the United States, mostly along the middle of the road.

WHAT'S ACTUALLY CHANGING

Beyond the increase in the number of states or commonwealths that have laws inclusive of sexual orientation and gender identity for the purposes of employment, housing, public accommodations, and credit, there are other very significant changes in our society on issues that involve sexual orientation and gender identity.*

---

*Not all of the laws cover the same things in the same ways in each of the fourteen states, but what they have in common is that they are all laws as opposed to executive orders, ordinances, or regulations and so carry the weight of litigation. I have chosen not to publish the names because it is likely that one or two more will be added to the list by the time this book appears, and just publishing numbers and percentages is difficult in this rapidly changing environment.

- The 2000 U.S. Census found 15 million self-identified gay/lesbian people and almost a million who self-identified as being part of a same-sex household, with or without children.[6] What is remarkable is not the numbers, because there is reason to think that it's an undercount. What's remarkable is that there was no box to check to indicate sexual orientation and/or partner status. These are people who just took it upon themselves to do so.
- Sixty-three percent of registered voters are in favor of civil unions for same-sex couples in the United States.[7]
- A plurality, or about 47 percent of Americans, favor full legal marriage for same-sex couples. In the group of people aged eighteen to thirty-five, this percentage jumps to more than 65 percent.[8]
- Eleven states bar, by executive order, discrimination against gay people in state employment. Only eight years ago, there were none.
- Gallup reported in December 2003[9] that 79 percent of all Americans believe that gay people should be allowed to openly serve in the military. In the eighteen-to-twenty-nine age range, 91 percent agreed with this position. In the thirty-to-forty-nine range, 81 percent agreed, and in the fifty-to-sixty-and-over age range, 70 percent agreed. These percentages also broke down to 73 percent of men and 85 percent of women responding in the affirmative. This was an increase of 15 percent over 2002 and 23 percent in 2001, when the affirmative responses for the total population were only 64 percent and 56 percent, respectively.
- Six out of ten (62 percent) heterosexual adults say that employees with same-sex partners should be equally eligible for key workplace benefits available to spouses of married employees in general. Approval for equitable benefits, when broken down into specific categories such as medical/dental benefits awarded without tax penalties, leave for same-sex employees on par with what heterosexuals can take advantage of as per FMLA, relocation benefits, and COBRA benefits, were all between 60 percent and 70 percent.[10]
- More than 7,000 organizations in the public, private, nonprofit, and university sectors offer domestic partner benefits to either same-sex only or same- and opposite-sex couples and their fam-

ilies. There were exactly 100 such organizations on January 1, 1992.

- The percentage of organizations that include the words "sexual orientation" in their nondiscrimination policies has increased 7 to 10 percent every year for the past ten years. Currently, 157 organizations (all sectors) also include "gender identity" or "gender identity/expression" in their nondiscrimination policies. Three years ago, there were less than twenty. Now this number comprises twenty-five of the Fortune 500 alone.[11]
- At least thirty states have adoption laws on the books or have a preponderance of legal decisions to support second-parent/step-parent adoption by same-sex couples.
- Forty-six states have adoption laws that allow people, regardless of sexual orientation, to adopt children if they are otherwise qualified to do so.
- Sodomy laws have been declared unconstitutional, signaling a growing awareness that sexual orientation is part of who you are, and not entirely what you do. Also, perhaps, that whatever it is you "do" is private, as long as it's between consenting adults.

What is behind the trend toward expanding the classifications of people who can take advantage of the civil and workplace rights that all Americans should be entitled to? I think it's this: In 1990, only about 25 percent of Americans reported having a gay friend or acquaintance. In 2000, that percentage was over 50 percent.[12] According to the Gill Foundation in 2003, the percentage of straight people who say they know at least one gay person is 90 percent.[13] And findings from the Human Rights Campaign (HRC) Public Report from February 2004 show that more than 60 percent of gay/lesbian people are out to even their casual acquaintances and co-workers.[14]

The truth seems to be that actually knowing someone who is gay makes it just about impossible for all but the seriously unyielding among us not to understand that people are people, and that being gay, lesbian, bisexual, asexual, or straight is simply a part of who a person is. It carries no more weight or importance relative to political beliefs or morality or character for a gay person than it does a straight person. It just is.

The data support the conclusion that seizing every opportunity to be as inclusive as possible is not only good for the individual and the collective psyche; it's also undisputedly good for the bottom line. To this point, Professor Richard Florida, of Carnegie Mellon University, and Gary Gates, a demographer at the Urban Institute, released data from a study they did in May 2003.[15] Some of their conclusions follow:

- New ideas and cutting-edge industries that lead to sustained prosperity are more likely to exist where gay people feel welcome.
- Most centers of tech-based business growth also have the highest concentration of gay couples. Conversely, major metropolitan areas with few gay couples tend to be slow- or no-growth places. They cited Pittsburgh and Buffalo as having low percentages of gay couples and also as being two of the only three major regions of the United States to lose population between 1990 and 2000.
- Innovation and economic vitality are closely associated with the presence of gay people and other overt indicators of acceptance and diversity such as a high percentage of immigrants and the level of racial and ethnic integration.
- Creative, innovative and entrepreneurial activities tend to flourish in the same kinds of places that attract gays and others outside the norm.

According to Florida, more than a few heterosexuals look for a "visible gay community as a signal of a place that's likely to be both exciting and comfortable. . . . They are looking for signs that nonstandard people, and ideas, are welcome."

This is an incredibly powerful quote and set of data because it reinforces what many believe about people and how they like to be treated. We want to see signs that the places where we reside and work acknowledge us. Furthermore, people want to know that if they exhibit creativity, innovation, or thinking outside of the box then they aren't going to get slapped down for it. Places that exhibit an acceptance of diversity are more likely to also be places that will accept innovations of thought and action. This frees people and allows them to put forth their best effort. Isn't that, in the end, the entire point?

THE LANGUAGE USED IN THIS BOOK

You will find that I use the word *gay* to refer to people who are not heterosexual without, sometimes, regard for their sex (male or female) or orientation (homosexual, bisexual, or asexual). I don't now, and really never did, subscribe to the use of the words homosexual (unless specifically being used in a clinical reference), lesbian, or queer. This last is for reasons I alluded to earlier; it strikes me as a very negative and argumentative term that also seems to be a rallying cry for separateness and the politicizing of sexual orientation. I've no desire to encourage separateness or to politicize sexual orientation. Enough people are out there doing both.

In the past three or so years, the LGB, which stood for "lesbian, gay, bisexual," was expanded to include "T" for "transgender." As we'll see in the chapters about sexual-orientation and gender-identity education, this is not actually correct, but it's not a problem in my opinion either.

Then the LGBT occasionally had an "S" attached to it for "straight." This is more correct than adding the T, and it doesn't happen often enough in my opinion. I'll repeat myself on this point too, I'm sure, but if the subject is sexual orientation (and it is), then straight people should always be included.

I've noticed recently that LGBTS is now sometimes LGBTQI; the Q is for queer and the I is for intersexual. Sometimes the Q is for "questioning." I have never seen this expanded acronym include the S for straight people and it's also, frankly, where I got off this particular train. So, in this book the acronym will be LGBTS.

You may wonder why I shy away from the word *lesbian*. The word derives from the Greek island of Lesbos, where, it is said, in the sixth century B.C., resided a "warrior princess" named Sappho (think Xena without the special effects) whose job was to do the dirty work of the emperor or whoever hired her and her army of women. Simply put, they were mercenaries. In her off hours, Sappho ran a school for the young women and wrote poetry that concerned itself (or some of it did) with love between women. So, from this we get lesbian because they lived on Lesbos.

The word has a legitimate etymology, but I find it stifling. First, I am not Greek and I don't like Sappho's poetry (perhaps because I was forced to read a lot of it in a college fine arts class). Second, the implication of the "lesbian" label is that one's attractions, intimacies, and friendships are exclusively with other women. This is limiting beyond belief and contributes to the myth of the "man-hating lesbian."

Third, the word has been adopted by some nonheterosexual women (emphasis on "some") to purposefully create a separateness between themselves and (1) other women who are not nonheterosexual, (2) men, regardless of sexual orientation, (3) anyone who doesn't view sexual orientation as a political issue.

I am well aware, however, that some women use no other term, and so occasionally I'll use it in this text. However, if I don't use it it doesn't mean that I'm talking only about men unless I specify this.

The word *homosexual* was first used by Karl Maria Kertbeny in 1869 in Prussia when arguing for the repeal of that country's anti-homosexual laws. Another term that was used in the late nineteenth century and around the turn of the twentieth century was *sexual inversion* or, when describing a person, *sexual invert,* the implication being one who "turns upside-down" or makes "opposite" the standard position of a thing.

Homo referring to *same* is an accurate enough word to use in describing a person's orientation and what it portends, but the term itself is rather stilted and long with a preponderance of misunderstanding assigned to it already, not to mention the degree of oversimplification it lends to something that is not so simple. Besides, Elton John is the only one who seems to pronounce it with any degree of class, and who in their right mind wants to mess with Sir Elton?

People on both sides of the language question feel vehemently about the words used to describe them, and I am not only asked in sessions all the time about the right word to use but also called to task when I don't use "the right word."

The answer is, there is no right word, because there are people who can—and do—make an argument for their own choice. There are however, in my opinion, very definitely wrong words to use when describing a person by his or her sexual orientation. Two that come to mind are *dyke* and *fag.* True, some women and men have adopted these terms and use them freely as self-identifiers, sources of pride, signals of community, or even affectionately among friends. But for the most part we have not matured or progressed enough as a society to be able to use these mostly derogatory terms peacefully, so I don't recommend that others do, outside a knowing community or small circle of friends.

Therefore, I'll use the word *gay* to refer to nonheterosexual people and the word *straight* to describe heterosexual people in the hope that my readers will find both words friendly, easy to read, and generally enveloping of whatever aspect of sexual orientation I am writing about at the time.

In fairness to many, many people who have asked me if I know where the word *gay* comes from in terms of its reference to homosexuality, I have to admit that I still can't say with absolute certainty. However, I have done some additional digging for this edition, and this is what I've discovered: Use of the word *gay* is said to predate Kertbeny's coining of *homosexual,* but no one seems able to document that. Evidence of its use, primarily in the gay subculture, can be traced as far back as the 1920s in both European and American cities, but there is nothing specific to prove this. There was a time, but only in the 1960s, when people thought *gay* meant and was derived from "good as you."

It's thought that the earliest usage of the word in print was from a Gertrude Stein story called "Miss Furr and Mrs. Skeene," published by *Vanity Fair* in 1922. The references in Stein's story appeared as, "They were . . . gay, they learned little things that are things in being gay . . . they were quite regularly gay." No one can say for sure whether Stein was referring to lesbianism or just that these two women were happy. I don't know; I've never read the story myself, but like most people who've studied literature to any extent, I have heard the stories about Stein and her various relationships.

The first unequivocal written use of gay to mean homosexual is in Ford and Tyler's *Young and Evil* (1933). In the 1938 Cary Grant/Katherine Hepburn movie *Bringing Up Baby,* Grant's character, David, is asked why he is wearing women's clothing. "Because I just went gay all of a sudden" is his reply. In their 1941 book *Sexual Variations,* Gershon Legman and G. V. Henry cite the word *gay* as a slang term for homosexual. The fact that it's included in their book in the 1940s indicates the word had been used in that way for some time prior to then.

Another explanation is that the word derives from gaycat or "geycat," which was slang for a hobo or a tramp new to life on the road. Gaycats were typically in the company of older tramps, which implied a homosexual relationship. This theory makes some sense if only because the term and the life were both in vogue in the 1890s.

THE REST OF THIS BOOK

Chapter 2 provides an overview of strategies you can employ to engender inclusion of sexual orientation and gender identity in this ever-changing world. Some of the strategies touched upon in Chapter 2 deserve, and get, their own chapters later in the book. Education specific to sexual orientation, education specific to gender identity, the responsibilities and contributions of employee networks, and leveraging your commitment to inclusion in the marketplace are covered in Chapters 4, 5, 6, and 7, respectively.

Chapter 3 is about the importance of really knowing the meaning of certain words, which is important when working in or discussing these aspects of human diversity. It also covers organizational coming out and offers facts to replace myths that continue to persist around gay and transgender people.

Chapter 8 looks at domestic partner benefits, civil unions, and same-sex marriage. More than any other chapter in the book, this one demands that a range of alternatives be explored, because same-sex marriage is a reality now in Europe (Belgium, the Netherlands), Canada, and the United States (Massachusetts). Whether these marriage rights will expand to other countries and/or states remains to be seen. But marriage applied to same-sex couples will affect many aspects of DP benefits going forward.

Finally, Chapter 9 looks at sexual orientation and gender identity in the schools. It explores not only issues of importance to gay and transgender youth but also the ways in which education syllabi are being changed and expanded to include sexual orientation and gender identity.

Five appendixes provide additional resources in the form of bibliography, organizations, examples of assessment interrogatories, and more information for transgender people going through or contemplating transition while continuing to work.

IT'S A MOVING TARGET

Honestly, I've seen more positive movement in issues that affect me as a gay person in this society during the past three years than I ever thought I'd see in my whole life. I never thought I'd see states with civil rights laws that take me into consideration; I never thought it would be possible that I'd marry; I never thought I'd see *Will & Grace* or *Queer Eye for the Straight Guy.* I'm not saying I like these shows; it's just significant in my life that they exist.

As I write this book in the spring of 2004, I know that much of what I write now will be different when it comes out in 2005. For that reason, I've shied away from providing counts of things such as the number of companies with nondiscrimination policies, or naming states that have this law or that. Instead, I talk about trends, movement, progress, and, sometimes, backlash.

What I know will be the same, still viable and still necessary in 2005 and probably for years to come, is information provided in good faith that seeks to illuminate and inform people on subjects that this society still seems to have so much trouble with. I know that subjects such as education, benefits, and marketing opportunities will be as important in a year as they are now, and I hope people find the information I provide helpful and useful.

Chapter 2

Strategies for Inclusion
in the New World

On January 29, 2004, The Journal Register News Service in Rhode Island put out a story about a six-month study that had been conducted by John Snow, Inc. of Boston on behalf of Equity Action and the Rhode Island Foundation called Meet the Neighbors.[1] The study found that despite having good educations, good jobs, and being more generous with their money and time to charitable and volunteer organizations, gays, lesbians, and other people with nonstandard gender identities are regularly discriminated against, in some cases daily, in schools, workplaces, and places of public accommodation.

The survey, which inquired of 371 LGBT people in the Providence, Rhode Island, area reported the following:

- One in ten respondents said they experienced or witnessed homophobia or discrimination in the workplace at least monthly.
- One in three suffers discrimination on the street and/or a public establishment.
- Ten percent experience some form of discrimination by professionals.

In the past three to five years similar surveys have been conducted in major and minor metropolitan areas throughout the United States. I chose this one because it was dated 2004, but by the time this book appears there will be others, thanks in part to all of the polling and opinion gathering that will go on in response to the debate over same-sex marriage. In case you are wondering if the data would be any different from other parts of the country, consider that the Rhode Island report comes out of the so-called liberal Northeast. Boston remains one of the last holdout cities regarding allowing an LGBT Irish group to march in its St. Patrick's Day parade. The only place I was ever personally verbally gay-bashed myself (aside from some of the truly amazing—and rude—things people have found it necessary to say to me during a class or presentation) was in Provincetown, Massachusetts, a well-known gay mecca where it's one out of ten people who are straight. Go figure.

I've had people tell me that I can never hope to do the work that I do with any success in any place south of the Mason-Dixon Line, but I've never found that to be the case. They will refer to the Bible Belt, but as near as I can tell that belt is as wide as the whole country because I've never been to a place in the United States where people didn't wear their religion on their sleeve. Be that as it may, I've also never been to a place where even those who make it a point to somehow communicate to me right off the bat that they are "Christian" or "religious" or "scripture readers" were also completely closed minded. I've had both wonderful and frustrating experiences doing this work all over the United States, and I have learned never to preconceive of the welcome that either I or what I have to say is going to get.

If I wanted to, I could write a book consisting of nothing but data from such polls as the Kaiser or Rhode Island efforts going back as far as 1980, but the results would always be the same in terms of progress and backlash and the discrimination that some people face on just about a daily basis. This is not to say that nothing has changed for the better, because it certainly has. But a great deal more work must be done to ensure not only equitable civil liberties for all but also safe and productive workplaces for all.

WHAT THE WORK IS FOR

Louise Young, cochair of the Human Rights Campaign Business Council in the late 1990s, developed a simple formula to estimate the cost of an inequitable workplace.[2] Her formula assumes a 5 percent nonheterosexual population, which I think is too conservative, but I do understand why she'd choose to be conservative in her estimates. For this edition, I choose to use what I believe is a more realistic—although also very conservative—10 percent. Ms. Young used 10 percent to estimate the amount of productivity associated with a safe and equitable workplace, and I continue to use that percentage as well.

Using her model with these percentages, a company employing 5,000 people has 500 people who are not heterosexual. If the average salary is $40,000 and the average loss of productivity per nonheterosexual worker is $4,000 ($40,000 × 10 percent = $4,000), then the annual loss to the company is estimated to be $2 million.

Take Microsoft, for example. When implementing domestic partner benefits, Microsoft said publicly that it believes *each* employee the company loses to the competition or to less-than-optimum productivity is worth $2 million over the estimated average "lifespan" of a Microsoft employee. Using their own calculations, if they lost the productivity of 10 percent of their workforce due to a less-than-equitable workplace, their losses would skyrocket into the billions of dollars. Given their annual revenue and scope of products, this is not an unreasonable estimate.

People do not work at their best if they work in fear, but data show that fear is still prevalent. Not only can we point to studies such as the one from Rhode Island noted earlier but, for example and as directly related to the workplace, in 2001 the Kaiser Family Foundation reported that 93 percent of self-identified GLB people are open about their orientation with heterosexual friends, but only 55 percent with their bosses.[3] These numbers are collaborated by the 2004 HRC Public Report as generated by Witeck-Combs Communications.[4] In a section of this report about how open LGBT adults are with various people or groups of people in their lives, they found that while 93 percent of the total sample of LGB people are out to close friends, 72 percent to siblings, 68 percent to parents, and 60 percent to co-workers, only 55 percent are out to their boss/manager.

Now, some readers will cry foul because I used these very same statistics in Chapter 1 to demonstrate that increased awareness of LGBT people in their lives is changing attitudes of heterosexuals for the better. And I meant it. Now I'm saying that relationships with bosses and managers pale in comparison to those that gay people have with other important people in their lives, and that's a bad thing. Until the percentages show that well over 90 percent of LGB Americans are out of the closet period, these percentages will be a double-edged sword. It swings both ways, and I want people to understand that.

Another set of data released by Witeck-Combs, this one in late 2003, reported that, generally speaking, six out of ten heterosexual adults think that people in committed, same-sex relationships should get the same workplace benefits as heterosexual, married couples.[5] I used this in Chapter 1 too. Here's what I didn't use in that chapter and it just reinforces why these statistics have to be viewed with regard to how they manifest in the real world.

For the second year in a row, while Witeck-Combs and others were touting the increased openness of LGBT issues at work and in the world and the resulting progress made in other people's attitudes, LGBT Americans continued to report little change in the level of discrimination they have witnessed or personally experienced. Four of ten LGBT Americans said they have faced some form of discrimination on the job, including being fired, harassed, pressured to quit, or denied a promotion because of their sexual orientation or gender identity. Also, more heterosexuals (52 percent) reported hearing jokes about LGBT people than they did in 2002 (45 percent).

All of the closeted employees I've interacted with admitted worrying about being found out, to the extent that it negatively affects their performance every day. This is not good for the individual or for the organization. Hiding takes energy and time that should be spent on the task at hand.

GROUND RULES FOR THE WORK

Behavior, Not Beliefs

Two precepts guide the work that I do; they are my mantras. They are "behavior, not beliefs" and "education, not endorsement." I may harbor secret desires to have everyone agree with my point of view, believe as I believe, and think what I think, but those desires are not part of the work I do. They can't be. People have a funny habit of thinking for themselves, and it's that part of their nature that I focus on. I believe that if you give people good, factual information with an open mind and heart, they will receive at least some of it. Furthermore, I know that if you tell people what you are offering them is for their consideration and not some mandate, they actually do consider it. I've seen change in people's beliefs and I guess that's always made me feel somewhat gratified. But mostly I've seen people's behaviors toward LGBT individuals change, and that's gratifying enough.

Why do I approach the work this way? Because it's no more right for LGBT people or the organization to force their positions down the throats of those who disagree than it is to allow that disagreement to lead to any kind of workplace discrimination. None of us checks our orientation at the door any more than we check our convictions there. But we all enter into a common agreement about *behavior at work* in support of common goals, which are usually productivity and/or profitability.

There will no doubt be varying opinions about orientation, but when those opinions lead to argument or to discrimination, the organization can and must step in to make certain demands on the behaviors of its workers.

Some people ask me how the organization can, in fact, be inclusive of sexual orientation and gender identity issues in what they call "conservative environments." I use the following analogy to prove that difficult topics are handled in workplaces all the time, even those where the basis of the difficulty is religion.

The analogy has to do with abortion and abortion rights. Although neither abortion nor sexual orientation necessarily should be issues with political, religious, moral, sexual, and social implications, they both currently are. Abortion polarizes people, upsets many, disrupts lives, influences legislation, and has caused extreme violence. In short, it has similar effects on some people as sexual orientation.

Let's say that a given employee is "pro-life" on the abortion question, which I recognize is an oversimplification of a complicated position. But for the sake of this example, at work, all she does during free time is harangue her colleagues about abortion, about their need to protest it, about their need to sign petitions to outlaw it, about their need to pray about it, and so on.

Take a minute to put yourself in the place of her supervisor. Assume, again for the sake of the example, that your position is also, generally speaking, pro-life. But consider the effect that this constant harping, handing out of printed material, and urgings to march are having on your team's cohesiveness. Take a minute to consider the effect it's having not only on other "pro-life" members of your team but also on "pro-choice" members.

Faced with this predicament, what do you think you'd do? When I've presented this example to managers and supervisors throughout America for the past four or five years, the response was, almost without fail, that they would take that person aside and quietly, respectfully, and likely without divulging their own position on the subject, tell her to cool it, immediately, or risk disciplinary action for destroying a safe, productive, and profitable work environment for everyone.

The point is that orientation must be accorded this same level of validity and respect—on both sides of the issue. People's opinions at work can live in balance with their professional responsibilities to the organization and to everyone in it. *A person's convictions, whatever their basis, can never be allowed to interfere with the principles of creating a positive work environment for all.* If people, regardless of their positions at a company, cannot set aside some convictions in order to do their jobs and allow others to do theirs, then the company is entitled to offer information to help them bring their convictions in line with their responsibilities, typically in the form of education. Or they are entitled to leave and go where they believe the values of the organization are more in line with their own.

I've seen people leave the employ of an organization because it put nondiscrimination language that included orientation into its policy, or because the organization implemented domestic partner benefits. This rarely happens, but it does happen. Frankly, although I wish that some individuals didn't feel it necessary to quit their jobs just because I was educating on these topics in their workplaces, I actually have a great deal of respect for them for literally putting their money where their convictions are. But I respect the organizations more for letting them walk and for not letting a particular view result in discriminatory practices.

Education, Not Endorsement

The other mantra, *education, not endorsement,* refers to my faith in education as a means of getting people to think about things that they didn't previously think about because they were not armed with the necessary information or language. A big part of my program about sexual orientation focuses on the meaning of words such as "sexual orientation" (see Chapter 4) and also about "choice," "preference," and "lifestyle" and why it is incorrect to use them in conjunction with sexual orientation. I do not subscribe at all to the belief that a person's lifestyle is dictated in any way by sexual orientation. There is no gay lifestyle, and I can prove it simply by asking this question: what is the straight lifestyle? I've been asking people this question for a dozen years and have never gotten an answer, satisfactory or otherwise. Why? Because a person's sexual orientation does not determine his or her lifestyle. Resources and interests do. There is no gay lifestyle, or gay opinion, or gay way of looking at everything, just as straight people rarely, if ever, share these things. Therefore, nothing, no way of life or looking at it or dealing with it, is being endorsed when LGBT rights are endorsed.

If the information about the purpose of this type of diversity work and the ground rules are correctly and completely communicated, there is no reason why this work cannot be done in any workplace anywhere.

THE WORK

The strategies at your disposal to effectively deal with sexual orientation and gender identity in the workplace are

- nondiscrimination policies (Endorsing ENDA [Employment Non-Discrimination Act]),
- education,
- domestic partner benefits,
- employee networks/alliances—mentoring,
- marketing to the LGBT community,
- internal and external outreach, and
- knowledgeable internal resources and reference libraries.

Education, domestic partner benefits, employee networks, and marketing efforts all get their own chapters. In this chapter, I cover nondiscrimination policies, external outreach, and internal resources. I also provide information about what is necessary to make these strategies a success. I end by providing a set of tools and techniques that I have found useful and have been distributing to people for many years.

Nondiscrimination Policies

In 2000, 42 percent of Americans thought that sexual orientation was protected in a federal statute (although they couldn't say which). I don't know what the percentage is now, but I would guess that still more than one-third of all Americans believe this. The fact is that neither sexual orientation nor gender identity is part of any federal statute, code, or law from the Constitution to the Bill of Rights to any Civil Rights Act or Pregnancy Discrimination Act or even the Americans with Disabilities Act. Fourteen states have laws that extend workplace protections and a couple of hundred local jurisdictions (including states, cities, towns, counties) have executive orders or ordinances that refer to these matters. Only four states and about fifty other jurisdictions provide protections to people on the basis of gender identity.

What this means is that LGBTS people in thirty-six states and the majority of all jurisdictions have no protections under the law in terms of whether they can be fired or not hired in the first place just for being gay or straight, or can be denied credit or service in a hotel or a restaurant based on real or perceived sexual orientation. This is why a county seat in Tennessee almost got away with passing a law that no gay or lesbian people could live there, and if they were found living there, they could be locked up or thrown out . . . literally. Thankfully, people all over Tennessee and the United States made it clear that they disapproved of this hateful nonsense, but the point is that had the county passed the ordinance, it would have been legal. How ridiculous is that?

Furthermore, the government is free to discriminate against gay Americans who want to serve in the armed forces. Why don't gays just serve in silence and get on with it? For two reasons actually. First, the closet is hell and trying to perform and keep a secret such as this is unhealthy, unsafe, and unproductive. Second, the military insists its members swear an oath of truth and then, if they are gay, immediately asks them to lie. Don't ask, don't tell is not only unnecessary but also childish and stupid.

When an organization includes the words *sexual orientation* and/or *gender identity* in its nondiscrimination policies, it is not just blowing smoke. These policies matter as statements of intent by the organization. They say, "This is who we are, and this is how we intend to treat people who work here or with whom we become affiliated." Absent any other protections, people outside the mainstream look for these policies because more often than not these days, they're all they're going to get.

The other thing about nondiscrimination policies that really matters is that without inclusive ones, none of the other strategies can be tried or implemented. In Chapter 3, I discuss how organizations "come out" around issues of sexual orientation, and the first step in that process for them is acknowledging that not everyone who works for them is gay. If an organization won't even acknowledge the presence of a group of people, in this case gay and transgender people, by including them in their nondiscrimination policies, what makes them think they are going to improve the environment for everyone where these aspects of diversity are concerned?

Some organizations resist adding the words *sexual orientation* or, nowadays, *gender identity* to their policies because they fear that they will lose market share. They are afraid that having an inclusive policy will be interpreted as giving tacit approval and that customers who hold the opposite view will withdraw their business.

John M. Conley and William M. O'Barr, anthropologists at Duke University, responded to a hypothetical situation presented in the *Harvard Business Review*.[6] In this scenario, a valued employee of a financial services company notifies his boss that he intends to bring his same-sex partner to an upcoming corporate function at which clients will be present. The boss worries that in making his sexual orientation known, the employee may put some client relationships in jeopardy.

Conley and O'Barr maintained that it is neither economically necessary nor morally justifiable for organizations, even conservative ones, to "conform to the meaner aspects of their clients' cultures." For a long time, they point out, elite law firms insisted that the exclusion of women and racial minorities was justifiable because their clients just wouldn't stand for female or black lawyers. But in fact firms did start to diversify and the clients did stand for it.

An organization should not, according to these anthropologists, make the mistake of underestimating its customers. If institutions use their predictions of another's response as an excuse to not do what they know is right and is good business, they are missing the boat on the enormous opportunity to exercise the type of influence that can shape a culture and grab more market share. "We believe," they wrote, "that the history of elite law firms and others suggests that, in the long run, the moral choice is the lucrative one as well. When major changes in cultural values take place, it pays to be ahead of the trend rather than running behind making excuses."[7]

As of March 2004, 2,632 organizations include sexual-orientation language in their nondiscrimination policies. Seventy-five percent of the Fortune 500 is included in that number. Of these 2,632, 162 also include gender identity or gender identity/expression[8] (see Chapter 5 for clarification of this language).

Support for Public Policy

The strategy of supporting public policy that is inclusive of sexual orientation and gender identity goes hand in hand with what the organization does concerning its nondiscrimination policy, because if a federal law that included sexual orientation and gender identity existed, then the workplace would not be the only place people might go looking for some basic civil rights. Federal EEO pertains to race, sex, religion (and where is the separation of church and state here?), national origin, and color, while affirmative action pertains to minorities (undefined), women (who are actually the majority), disabled people (undefined), Vietnam-era veterans (but not veterans of other wars who may still be alive and working), or persons of other protected classes. Gay and transgender people are neither protected classes nor suspect classes and so fall outside any of these laws that protect employment rights specific to all aspects of the employment relationship, including but not limited to recruitment, hiring, promotion, transfer, layoff, compensation, and selection for training.

A question I've always asked myself when people complain about gay and transgender people wanting "special rights" because they're already included is, Where do they get that information? It is amazing to me that people who object to extending civil rights on the basis of sexual orientation and/or gender identity based on their religious beliefs can do so without laughing. Or maybe they are laughing, I don't know. The fact is, not only is freedom of (and from) religion guaranteed by the Constitution, it's also included in EEO policy and even occasionally included in the nondiscrimination policies of thousands of organizations. The same is true of race, sex, ethnicity, status as a veteran of Vietnam, or as a disabled person. Why do people get up in arms about adding sexual orientation to any of these when it's currently part of none of them? It's because they confuse "sex" as a verb with sexual orientation. They complain that gay people want special rights based on their sexual activity and their "lifestyle." Basically, they don't get it and some of them never will. They've got other fish they're trying to fry. Some of us are on to them.

If federal law is someday expanded to include sexual orientation and/or gender identity, it will not relieve organizations of the responsibility to continue including these aspects of diversity in their nondiscrimination policies, for the same reason that most, if not all, corporate nondiscrimination policies continue to include race or sex or gender. They are statements of intent; that intent will always need stating.

The Federal Government and ENDA

Why is it important that we have laws to protect people in this country? Because everything else seems to be at the whim of politics and that process cannot be trusted to preserve and protect human rights. As J. S. Mill wrote in *On Liberty* a couple of hundred years ago, checks and balances protect people from the will of the majority—tyranny of the prevailing opinion.

President Bill Clinton signed an executive order during his presidency that extended workplace protections to federal workers on the basis of sexual orientation. He did not include gender identity. To no one's great surprise, certainly not mine, the current Bush administration has decided to let that protection fall by the wayside and they've gone a step further. On March 17, 2004, in an article for the online newspaper, *365gay.com,*[9] Paul Johnson, the paper's Washington Bureau chief, explained that Special Counsel Scott Bloch, appointed by Bush in January 2004 for a five-year term, had decided that a 1978 law intended to protect employees and job applicants from adverse personnel actions does not cover gay and lesbian people. Bloch determined that although a gay employee would have no recourse for being fired or demoted just for being gay, that same worker could not be fired for attending a gay pride event. Bloch maintains that gays and lesbians cannot be covered as a protected class because they are not protected under the nation's civil rights laws. What he conveniently glosses over, of course, is that gay people are not covered under the nation's civil rights laws because they are not a protected or suspect class (as the Constitution would put it). It's a catch-22 in the hands of a person who clearly has a political and social agenda he's trying to pound home on behalf of an administration that is in no way above pandering to the lowest common denominator in their so-called base.

Bloch was a busy man in his first three months as special counsel. In that time, he also managed to remove references to sexual-orientation discrimination from the OSC (Office of Special Counsel) complaint form, the OSC basic brochure, training slides, and a two-page flier titled "Your Rights As a Federal Employee."

Clearly, civil rights for LGBT people cannot be left solely to the politicians, which is why another strategy at the disposal of organizations is to endorse the Employment Non-Discrimination Act, or ENDA, and a federal hate crimes bill inclusive of sexual orientation and gender identity.

ENDA

This act has been floating around Congress for about five years now. It would

- extend to sexual orientation federal employment discrimination protections currently provided based on race, religion, sex, national origin, age, and disability;
- block public and private employers, employment agencies, and labor unions from using an individual's sexual orientation as the basis for employment decisions, such as hiring, firing, promotion, or compensation;
- allow for the same procedures and similar, but somewhat more limited, remedies as permitted under Title VII and the Americans with Disabilities Act; and
- apply to Congress, with the same procedures as provided by the Congressional Accountability Act of 1995, and presidential employees, with the same procedures as provided under the Presidential and Executive Office Accountability Act of 1996.

ENDA would not

- cover small businesses with fewer than fifteen employees;
- cover religious organizations, including educational institutions substantially controlled or supported by religious organizations (the bill covers only employees whose duties pertain solely to a

religious organization's activities which generate profits deemed taxable by the Internal Revenue Service);

- apply to the uniformed members of the armed forces, and thus not affect current law on lesbians and gay men in the military;
- allow for quotas or preferential treatment based on the sexual orientation of the individual;
- allow a disparate impact claim such as is available under Title VII of the Civil Rights Act of 1964;
- allow the imposition of affirmative action for a violation of this act;
- allow the Equal Employment Opportunity Commission (EEOC) to collect statistics on sexual orientation or compel employers to collect such statistics; or
- apply retroactively.

About 100 organizations have endorsed ENDA so far. Many don't know the legislation exists, but as with legislation that's been rolling around the Senate and the House regarding changing the tax code related to domestic partner benefits, I have a sneaking suspicion that this legislation is going to get plenty of publicity in 2005. Any organization that claims to be fully inclusive needs to take a long look at this act and then, hopefully, help get it passed.

Tips to Get Nondiscrimination Language in Policy and Law

If your organization does not currently include the words *sexual orientation* in its nondiscrimination policy, you can take steps to persuade it to do so. (Note: If the words in the policy are *preference* and/or *lifestyle* instead of *orientation,* the same strategies of promoting complete understanding and enlisting support on a peer level are still necessary.)

- Get a copy of the existing policy, review it with members of a gay/straight employee group, and make sure that it is completely understood. If no such group exists, review it with like-minded individual employees.

- If there are other employee groups sanctioned by the company, go to their meetings and try to engender their support for the language change.
- Try to identify a "champion" in senior management who is willing to listen to and present your concerns to the person(s) who can change the policy. Be prepared to have several discussions with this individual so that she or he is fully armed with the facts needed to solicit the change.
- Focus on the business case; if it were just a matter of right versus wrong, it would have happened already.
- Find out what the laws or executive orders are in your state or county. If your organization does business throughout the United States, you need to know what the laws/orders are in all of them so that you know how to position the policy statement for every place your organization operates.
- Unionized people have done very well in bringing this request to their representatives in order that it become part of a collective bargaining agreement.
- Never lose your sense of humor . . . you're going to need it!

If you are able to get the language added, the policy should

- be as clear as possible about what constitutes discrimination and that it won't be tolerated in any form;
- be widely publicized in all media where the current policy is published (there should be no policy "opt-outs" for inclusion of sexual orientation and/or gender identity); and
- make sure that any employee knows how to report an instance of discrimination covered by the policy.

Internal and External Outreach Strategies

Some internal outreach strategies are intrinsic to the creation and ongoing success of an employee alliance or network, so some of what's here may appear in Chapter 6, which is all about employee groups.

Internal outreach means ensuring that all communication uses inclusive language and that all people, regardless of background, are made to feel welcome.* It means supporting the constructive efforts of a sanctioned group by making sure they have the same access to budget and technology as do other employee networks. In too many organizations with which I've worked, the women's group, to use a broad example, is a national effort, while the gay/straight alliances operate regionally. The message being sent here is clear to those involved and speaks of a basic hypocrisy of policy that eats away at the ability to make progress. If all your employee alliances are regional, then fine; but if they are all national except one or two, then that is not fine.

In this day and age, it's also very important that all employee groups have equitable use of and access to internal electronic bulletin boards or intranets as a way of publicizing events or engendering communication among members. Again, if some groups have full access to these systems and some groups don't, this doesn't send the right message.

Internal outreach also means doing everything possible to encourage participation by all types of people in the organization and going out of the way, perhaps far out of the way, to work to provide a safe environment where closeted gay people can come out or participate in any way that feels safe to them. It is all too common that nonheterosexuals at the headquarters' facilities or in urban centers feel affirmed and valued and able to be out while their co-workers at more distant facilities work and live in fear for their lives.

Community outreach means getting involved in some of what is going on in the communities in which you operate. It means supporting local organizations such as PFLAG[10] or endorsing ENDA to Congress. It also means allowing your employees to participate in community speaking programs and/or to work on behalf of your company in support of Meals on Wheels programs or the fight against breast and ovarian cancer. Put more than your money out there; give people the opportunity to represent you in these causes in their community. The PR you'll get from this will be well worth the negligible expense.

Cooperation with other organizations, especially in terms of best practices, can be extremely valuable, as can the sharing of technology

---

* A note about inclusive language: When I refer to this, I don't mean that organizations should stop using words such as *husband* or *wife*. There's nothing wrong with those words. A simple insertion of *partner* or, if you prefer, *significant other* signals to everyone that the organization is aware that, as of right now, not everyone has a husband or wife or even spouse as those terms are commonly understood today.

to support diversity initiatives in different cities. This strategy can also help to mitigate some of the fears associated with negative public relations from doing proactive things around aspects of diversity that are still considered untouchable by some people.

Knowledgeable Internal Resources and Reference Libraries

Make sure there is a resource room, kiosk, or person who is up to speed on all of what is going on relative to sexual orientation in every single facility that you maintain. People on all sides of the question need to have a place to go to get information instead of letting their concerns fester and eat away at their confidence and ability to perform their jobs.

A room or referral service should be set up in such a way that either can be accessed anonymously if an individual desires, although hopefully soon such anonymity won't be considered necessary. Such resources may be limited to existing employee assistance programs (EAPs) or could also include listings of literature available on the subject at hand, statistical information about sexual orientation, and names and phone numbers of organizations of all kinds—from clergy to political to family-focused or legal—that offer support or information mechanisms. Here too, the company intranet can, using links, be a terrific way to help employees get information while maintaining confidentiality.

The organization can also use a consultant as an information resource. Consultants can provide a single information source, or can refer employees to groups, counselors, schools, and other organizations that have expertise in the employee's area of concern.

Other strategies that the organization may want to consider spearheading include the following:

- A hotline to report all forms of harassment and discrimination including, but not necessarily limited to, sexual orientation
- A system of accountability for a nonhostile work environment by division, work group, business unit, geography, or other criteria
- Expansion of existing reward/award programs to include recognition of superior efforts to engender a safer, better working environment for all—with an emphasis, perhaps, on sexual orientation

- Encouragement of gay employees to bring their partners to appropriate enterprise-wide events, or to display (again, appropriately, as others do) items from their personal lives

If the organization and individuals therein adopt some or all of these strategies for inclusion, benefits will be reaped in terms of greater productivity that is the direct result of almost universal increased job satisfaction. Granted, there will be pockets of virulent resistance to change, and some people might leave. But those who stay will exhibit a higher degree of job involvement and organizational commitment, with less absenteeism and turnover. No one said it would be easy, but I have no qualms saying it will be worthwhile.

Requirements to Support the Strategies

A few factors are absolute requirements to ensuring that any of these strategies have at least a decent chance of succeeding. First among them, and paramount to success, is management support of any or all strategies tried. This support needs to be verbal, written, and in the form of management's actual physical presence whenever possible. This will send the message that a solid connection exists between organizational values and diversity in support of the business or organization goals.

Another requirement is the continual demonstration of commitment to the strategy or strategies adopted. These can't ever be positioned or perceived as fire drills; if they are, they are doomed to failure. Also, make sure that information about programs and policies is out there and easy to find.

I have worked with more than one organization that, upon deciding to implement domestic partner benefits, for example, buried all reference to them so deep in the open enrollment materials (which can be quite dense without any additional help) that even those of us who knew what we were looking for and where the information was supposed to be couldn't find it. Then they made the process of enrolling or having questions answered equally labor-intensive. This sends as bad a message as allowing some groups to post notices on the company intranet and denying that right to others.

Actively include members of your organization from across groups, geography, management, and so on. Especially where geography is concerned, today's technology makes this both easy and cost-effective. Instead of divergent initiatives in different places, have the same initiatives with the same standards in different places—one organization operating as one. Even education programs can be offered this way using Web conferencing technology.*

TOOLS AND TECHNIQUES

Finally, I'd like to include a summary sheet of tools and techniques that I distribute to participants, especially managers, of every program that I do. They usually get annoyed with me if I don't point out that they're there, or if I gloss over them . . . and I don't want anyone reading this book to be annoyed with me. So instead of putting them in an appendix as I do with the class materials, I thought I'd just put them front and center. I hope if anyone reading this has questions about any of these strategies, they won't hesitate to contact me. You can find me on the Internet at <www.common-grnd.com>.

1. Educate yourself about sexual orientation in order to formulate, and where necessary express, a position that balances one's own opinion with the change-agent behavior encouraged by the organization.
2. Try to avoid heterosexist assumptions; that is, don't assume that everyone you work with or come into contact with is heterosexual.
3. Share anything you've learned about human sexuality and homophobia that might encourage others to adopt productive behaviors.
4. Use inclusive language whenever possible in all communications.
5. Encourage gay and transgender co-workers to be part of the social groups you form at work, including bringing their partners to functions when appropriate.

---

*Web conferencing is becoming a very important part of collaboration strategy for companies all over the globe. For more information about how it can be used in your organization to support this, any other diversity initiative, or really any other aspect of your business that involves communication and collaboration, see *The Web Conferencing Book* (Spielman/Winfeld), AMACOM, 2003.

6. Take time to understand the local laws and ordinances that relate to sexual orientation and gender identity, and especially your organization's nondiscrimination policies. If you have questions about these policies, ask.
7. If you have questions about orientation, use organizational resources or resources on the Internet (see Appendix I) to try to get answers. Only with information can people make informed decisions.
8. Display items in your workspace, such as books, magnets, and posters, that demonstrate your awareness of inclusiveness.
9. If someone asks you a question or confronts you with an opinion about sexual orientation in the workplace that you feel unprepared for, feel free to say that you don't know how to respond, but that you will get back to her or him. Then reach out to the organizational resources available to you so that you can respond in a meaningful and helpful way.
10. Refuse to laugh at antigay humor.
11. Cite company policy about nondiscrimination, or simply walk away from a group that is indulging in verbal discrimination. If you feel comfortable doing so, personalize the issue by saying "I know gay people and what you just did/said offends me."
12. Encourage other people to read books or attend education sessions on sexual orientation in order to avail themselves of other points of view if they seem particularly troubled by the issue.

Chapter 3

The Facts of the Matter

There's a secret about doing work around diversity in the workplace that I'm about to share with you, even though some of my consultant colleagues will be angry that I let this particular cat out of the bag. The truth is that while we who consult and teach diversity topics seem always focused on the characteristics that make human beings different, the entire point is to prove that it is precisely all of those differences that make us exactly the same. When word gets out about this it's going to put us all out of business; but I'm not too worried, personally, that I won't be able to hang on until I decide to retire. Given the amount of time that we as a society have been grappling with issues such as race and gender, it's clear to me that there is still a great deal of work to be done, and sexual orientation is sure to be a conversation starter for years to come.

I chose the term *conversation starter* carefully, because I am convinced that a very large part of the difficulties experienced in the workplace—and perhaps also outside of it—concerning sexual orientation stems from a lack of knowledge about what it is. People don't, generally, talk about sexual orientation in any meaningful way because they seem to believe that in doing so they are talking about "privacy" or "sex" (as a verb) and such things are best not discussed.

They're wrong. Such things are best discussed. Without dialogue there is never any progress made on anything. Besides, discussions about sexual orientation, especially in the workplace, are not about privacy or sex. They are not about the way we conduct ourselves or the intimate aspects of our lives. They are about part of who we are, every single one of us.

IMPORTANT TERMS

Sexual Orientation

Sexual orientation is not "code" for "homosexuality." To make the mental translation of "sexual orientation = stuff about homosexual people," although common, is misinformed.

Sexual orientation is that which determines to whom you will, absolutely, become physically and/or emotionally attracted. Everyone has a sexual orientation; there are four of them:

- Heterosexuals are those who will, absolutely, become physically and/or emotionally attracted to those of the opposite sex.
- Homosexuals are those who will, absolutely, become physically and/or emotionally attracted to those of the same sex.
- Bisexuals are those whose capacity for physical and/or emotional attraction extends to either sex.
- Asexuals are those who do not become physically and/or emotionally attracted to others, regardless of the other's sex.

The level of attraction that is being discussed here is not casual; it is serious but it is not necessarily physically intimate. The use of the words *physical* and *emotional* are intentionally in place of the words *erotic* and *sexual*. This is because I've learned in the past dozen years that words such as *erotic* and *sexual* all by themselves make people uncomfortable. They get so wrapped up in them that they cannot hear the information that is intended to further their understanding about this aspect of human sexuality.

It's important to note here that sexual orientation is, in fact, a rung on what I call the ladder of human sexuality. The other rungs leading up to it are biological sex, gender identity, and gender role. Sexual orientation is followed up the ladder by sexual orientation identity. All of these terms and their relationships to one another are explained in more detail in Chapter 4 on specific education-program content.

So when the topic is sexual orientation in the workplace, it is not just "gay issues in the workplace" or education about gay, lesbian, bisexual, and transgender people. It is education about all people and the aspects of our work lives and interactions that are affected by our sexual orientation. That we are discussing all people, not just gay people, is a key point.

The distinction between casual and intimate attraction is important, as is the "and/or" in each definition of a sexual orientation. First, it's important to understand that we are talking about that level of attraction that causes people to sometimes do silly, weird, irresponsible, wonderful, or awful things. You're walking down the street on a perfectly nice day without a care in the world and feeling totally cool and together and then . . . you see her . . . or you see him . . . and all of a sudden, you forget where you're going or what you were thinking about. You can't remember what you did an hour ago, and you don't know why your palms are all sweaty or why you are starting to shake and feel dazed and confused. Congratulations. You're in love, or you're in lust. The stimulus if you are a heterosexual man is a woman. If you are a gay woman, it's also a woman. Maybe it's the same woman. If she sees and has the same reaction to both of you, perhaps she is a bisexual woman. The point is that this is the level of attraction to which I refer. You may have just fallen in love or maybe have been overcome with lustful desires toward that person, but either way, your capacity to feel that depth of desire is determined by your sexual orientation.

So this is not the same as when a woman comments to her husband that another woman who just passed them by on the street looks terrific in the suit she's wearing. Nor is it the same as men working out together in a gym who admire the physique of another man. It has nothing to do with old friends of the same sex who claim to love each other. There are all kinds of intimacy; the ones kicked off by our sexual orientation can only be described as special.

The fact is, most people don't know what you've just learned in the past couple of pages, but why would they? We don't talk about these matters. We don't talk about them precisely because most people don't know what you've just learned and most people, to their credit actually, don't go diving headlong into conversations about topics they feel ill-prepared to discuss. Because misconceptions about sexual orientation being wholly about gays, or matters of absolute privacy, or sexual behavior are rampant, people don't discuss it because they don't know, in the final analysis, what words to use.

If you don't feel as though you have a grasp of the terminology needed to discuss a given topic, chances are you won't discuss it. You wouldn't start arguing various economic policies intended to spur growth if you didn't understand what economic indicators are or what the difference is between a balance sheet and a stock option. The same is true with sexual orientation and gender identity. The key to moving these things forward toward meaningful inclusion is getting people to understand them enough to be able to push past the rhetoric and really discuss the salient points. From such discussion, understanding and progress grow.

Homophobia

Another important term to get straight, as it were, is homophobia.

If translated literally, the word means "fear of sameness," which is interesting of course since it certainly manifests as a fear of difference. It's vitally important to understand the meaning of this word and all of the biases on which it is constructed because unless you understand completely what it is, you can never hope to communicate with someone who is exhibiting a bias that is commonly labeled homophobic. I think it is as inappropriate and unconstructive to haphazardly accuse others of homophobia without knowing where it may be coming from as it is for them to make any assumptions about me simply because they know I'm gay.

The more typical definition of *homophobia* is "the irrational fear and hatred of homosexuals." This is pretty accurate in describing how the condition plays itself out. It is irrational in the sense that when reason and understanding are applied to sexual orientation, fear and hatred typically disappear. When fear and hatred disappear, constructive conversation is much more likely.

Homophobia, according to The Campaign to End Homophobia, comes in four types: personal, interpersonal, institutional, and cultural.[1] By combining these types with the three biases that, according to Dr. Gregory Herek of the University of California, cause homophobia, it is possible to get a very well-detailed and much more correct idea of what homophobia really is. The biases identified by Dr. Herek are experiential, defensive, and symbolic.[2]

Personal Homophobia

An individual's belief that gay people are sick, immoral, inferior to straight people, or incomplete as men or women is called *personal homophobia*. People who are personally homophobic are not always straight. Many people who are gay are intensely homophobic. This phenomenon is called "internalized homophobia," and it occurs in gay people who have been battered by their families or society for so long that they come to believe that they really are somehow deficient. People who suffer from internalized homophobia are the people in the workplace who remain closeted voluntarily—not because they fear what others will say, but because of their own misunderstanding and discomfort of and with themselves. It is a very unhealthy place to be.

Personal homophobia is caused by what Herek calls a "defensive bias." When people believe that the image they project does not satisfy that of a "real man" or a "real woman" (whatever those terms mean to that individual), and that they might be labeled gay because of it, this makes them defensive and leads to what is typically called personally homophobic behavior.

Interpersonal Homophobia

The fear, dislike, or hatred of people believed to be gay is called *interpersonal homophobia.* It is likely to show itself in the form of name-calling, verbal and physical harassment, or widespread acts of discrimination. Violent harassment of gays, also called "gay bashing" all too frequently results in death.

Homophobia, generally speaking, has long been considered "the last acceptable prejudice." This is ridiculous. There is no such thing as an acceptable prejudice, especially when that prejudice results in physical pain or injury. What is most disturbing about interpersonal homophobia is that it is usually taught. The good new is, this means it can be untaught.

It's important to point out that most people act out their interpersonal homophobia in ways that are not physically violent. But the mental and emotional violence they perpetrate on gay family members, friends, or co-workers is no less devastating. Relatives who shun or vilify their gay parents, children, siblings, or other relatives; a military that casts aspersions on a person's desire and ability to serve her or his country; or a workplace that does not acknowledge the requirements of those with a nonmajority orientation all wreak devastating emotional cruelty on those affected.

Herek believes that one cause of interpersonal homophobia—whether expressed with physical or mental violence—is an experiential bias. This arises when a person who has had a bad experience with any type of person (or animal or thing) projects that experience to all people of the same type.

In other words, if a woman is approached by a gay female friend or acquaintance in a way that makes her feel uncomfortable, she may assume from that point on that all gay women will try to approach her that way. To understand how illogical this reaction is, she has only to think of her experience with men. In all likelihood she has at some point spurned the inappropriate advances of a male without concluding that all men will approach her in similarly inappropriate ways.

The second possible cause for interpersonal homophobia, according to Dr. Herek, is a symbolic bias that is driven by the belief that "homosexuality" destroys closely held value systems. Our values and belief systems help each of us get through this life, and we can react badly to whatever we feel threatens them. Symbolic biases drive some organizational efforts, hiding under cloaks of heightened morality, to attempt to scapegoat all gay people for the ills in the world.

Institutional Homophobia

Governments, businesses, churches, and other institutions of society discriminate against people because of their sexual orientation in many ways. This phenomenon is known as *institutional homophobia.* The organizations and institutions set policy, allocate resources, and maintain both written and nonwritten standards for their members. In the workplace, not listing sexual orientation in a nondiscrimination policy is institutionally homophobic. Not giving equal access to benefits and resources or the organization to (same-sex) partners is too. Not using inclusive language such as *partner* or not including unmarried significant others (same-sex) in invitations to corporate events is another example. Insisting that perceived cost increases, administrative complications, or outsiders are blocking the implementation of domestic partner benefits or saying that they are not needed outside of legal marriage are all also frequent examples of ongoing institutional homophobia.

The bias involved in institutional homophobia is, more often than not, symbolic.

Cultural Homophobia

Heterosexism is another term for cultural homophobia, a largely unstated but prevalent belief that everyone is straight or ought to be. This standard is reinforced in almost every TV show or print advertisement, where virtually every character is straight and every romantic or sexual relationship is heterosexual. This is starting to change, and more realistic and less stereotypical portrayals of nonheterosexuals are now present in the media, but no one has yet seen fit to allow a gay character to have a realistic love life. That was true when I first wrote that sentence in 1998, and it's still true in 2005.

In the workplace, heterosexism and its symbolic bias are at the root of many of the molehills that become mountains in the minds of people who think that progressive policies toward their gay employees will be detrimental to the organization.

History proves that no system of government or commerce, from slavery in ancient Egypt to slavery in nineteenth-century North America to slavery in twenty-first-century developing economies, survives if it is based on the misguided belief that one group is superior to another. It cannot because people who are discriminated against are unable to give their tasks their full effort and concentration. Nor are they able to reap the full benefits of their labor. And no group of people will put up with these inabilities indefinitely, especially when it becomes clear to them that they can initiate change. For gay people, this becomes clearer every day.

Without full knowledge of what sexual orientation and homophobia are—and what they are not—progress on these aspects of work and social life are impossible. However, with such knowledge, anything is possible.

COMING OUT: INDIVIDUALS
TO ORGANIZATIONS AND BACK

People do not work at their best if they work in fear. But prevalent homophobia and heterosexism in the workplace still induce many gay people to hide their sexual orientation and stay in the closet. Consider these facts from the Kaiser Family Foundation Studies on Sexual Orientation in the Workplace 2001.[3]

- Ninety-three percent of self-identified LGB people are open about their orientation with heterosexual friends, but only 55 percent with their bosses.
- More than 62 percent of LGB people make or have made important decisions about their lives and work based on their non-majority orientation.
- More than 75 percent of the gay population has experienced or known someone who experienced discrimination in applying to college, applying for a job, buying/renting a house, trying to get insurance, or trying to serve in the military.
- Seventy-five percent of all LGBT people have been the victim of verbal abuse at some point in their lives.

From my own experience, there is not an LGBTS employee group anywhere in the United States that doesn't maintain two membership lists—one for those who are openly involved, attend meetings and symposiums, and take on action items, and one for those who want to remain informed and who get involved on a very carefully chosen, case-by-case basis.

A principal goal of any organization should be to create a culture in which each employee has the opportunity to make a full contribution and to advance on the basis of performance. Hiding forces gay employees to lead a double life, to pretend that the things that motivate them to succeed on the job—their partner, their family, their home, their interests—don't exist. Organizations that continue to exclude segments of their workforce are sending the message that some people are less valued, less important, and less welcome.

Hiding in Plain Sight

Consider this for a moment. What would everyone do if gays couldn't hide? Women and racial minorities, who are also historic victims of workplace discrimination, did not have the luxury of hiding even if they wanted to. If gays couldn't hide, just as people of color and women could not hide, then all the questions surrounding them would come to a head that much faster.

It is the sheer ability for gay people to hide, to blend in, that makes some people believe that we choose to be as we are (because we can hide it practically on demand), and makes others believe that our arguments for equal rights are not as valid as those coming from people whose circumstances make it impossible to hide, as if logically it mattered. It's really become a "damned if you do, damned if you don't" situation. It's become untenable for most gay people to continue playing the game for two reasons. First, it's a losing game for the participant no matter what; it's unhealthy, unsafe, and a waste of time and energy. Second, as more people come out, especially in the workplace, and gain victories in equal employment provisions, among other things, it encourages more people to come out.

Being in the closet means censoring thoughts, words, and actions relative to one's sexual orientation all the time and with everyone you meet. A gay man may be in the closet to his family but not to his co-workers—or only to some of them. Perhaps a gay woman's brother knows the truth of her sexual orientation, but another brother, two sisters, her parents, and all the aunts, uncles, and cousins, save one who lives in Alaska, don't know. It can all be quite a handful to manage, and it becomes unmanageable fast, which is a large part of the reason that, in short order, gay people stop trying.

Don't believe me? Try it yourself. See if you can go through a whole day without doing, saying, demonstrating, wearing, displaying, or commenting upon anything that would send a signal to any other person that you come into contact with what your sexual orientation is. Most straight people can't go twenty minutes till their first slip. Give it a sincere try.

It is undoubtedly easier today than at any point in the past to be out of the closet in many parts of the United States and Canada. Unfortunately, it's not easy or possible in all parts of North America, but it is a goal worth striving for. The necessity for being out and being accepting for both individuals and organizations is tantamount to absolute. When looking for a job, more young people are asking themselves, "Will the new work environment be supportive of me as a member of an orientation or gender identification minority?" Most universities have nondiscrimination policies that are fully inclusive, and most of the top business schools in the United States, including many state systems, have domestic partner benefits. Today, more graduating students are out of the closet and they won't be going back in. If they feel that a certain employer will force them back into the closet through subtle but exclusionary practices, they will go somewhere else to work.

ORGANIZATIONAL COMING OUT

In the first two editions of *Straight Talk About Gays in the Workplace* we included content about how individuals come out. I still believe that there are three stages of coming out for people—comparison, support, and incorporation—but I also still believe that if you had ten gay men and/or women in a room and you asked them what their coming-out story was, you'd get ten different responses. I also believe that coming out is something that anyone can relate to and that it's not always about revealing a nonheterosexual orientation. The difficulties inherent in coming out of the closet should be apparent to anyone who's ever had a secret they were desperately afraid would be found out. Deciding to be honest with anyone or everyone in your life can sometimes be a painful and difficult challenge. It is always a personal decision.

More relevant to our discussion of orientation and gender identity in the workplace is the theory that Sue and I first had about ten years ago that organizations go through a coming-out process too. This process is still vitally important to the ways in which a given organization chooses to deal—or not—with policies and programs specific to workplace diversity that are (or are not) inclusive of sexual orientation. As such, and because I've expanded it just a little, it bears including in this edition.

First, make no mistake that coming out is a process for both individuals and organizations; it is not a pronouncement that occurs once. It is the act of realizing something and then letting that realization manifest itself in all aspects of a person's or organization's existence.

Homophobia in all its manifestations would be greatly reduced if more people only knew how many of their friends, acquaintances, coworkers, and family members are nonheterosexual. To the extent that every person—and organization—in the world will be able to come out of the closet, there will be (1) no more closeted gay people, (2) no more discriminatory workplaces, and (3) no more homophobia.

These are lofty goals, to be sure, and difficult. But they are attainable. I'm not naive, but if I did not believe in the indefatigable capacity for things to improve, for understanding to become more widespread, for positive change to eventually occur, and for people to be better tomorrow than they are today, I couldn't even get up in the morning.

Phase 1: Acknowledgment

Gay people are in every workplace. There are gay doctors, gay pilots, gay stockbrokers, gay lawyers, gay teachers, gay athletes, gay everybodies. In the acknowledgment phase, the organization states both verbally and in writing that it knows there are gay people in the world. In other words, it stops saying "We don't have any issues of sexual orientation to deal with because there are no gays working here."

Organizational acknowledgment carries with it the same positive force as an individual's acknowledgment of his or her own orientation or of someone else's. It says, "I acknowledge your existence, and although I might not always agree with you or even like you, I will not pretend that you are not here." Unfortunately, too many organizations continue to pretend that gay people don't exist within them or exist only in numbers too small to matter. I find that last sentiment particularly difficult to assimilate; how many of any kind of person does it take for an organization to want them to know, individually and as a group, that they are valued?

Phase 2: Accommodation

In the accommodation phase, the organization as a unit and all its individual cogs agree that specific provisions must be made to support their acknowledgment. So they begin to do things such as offering partner benefits to same-sex (and possibly to unmarried opposite-sex) couples. They use inclusive language in their communications, substituting the word *partner* for the word *spouse*. They reprimand (and mean it) those who discriminate or harass their colleagues, they put gay members on appropriate task forces, and they recognize gay employee groups (if other employee groups are similarly recognized). In short, they back up their acknowledgment with concrete action whenever possible. In this phase, the employer may have to be lobbied to be inclusive, but once (or twice) asked, it will.

Phase 3: Incorporation

In the final phase of organizational coming out, the employer does not need to be asked anymore, and no one individual working there has to wonder at all what is expected of him or her as regards his or her behavior toward gay co-workers.

Incorporation in an organization is just like incorporation in an individual. Sexual orientation is a fact of life. It just is. It is the result of a completely internalized understanding of the fact that people are people with lots of differing characteristics, of which sexual orientation is just one. An incorporated organization, again like an individual, is one that keeps its value judgments to an absolute minimum and strives to build in proactive correction systems for those times when negative judgments are made despite best efforts to avoid them.

Such organizations are marked by their progressive, proactive stances as reflected in everything they do. These organizations make it clear that an entity is only as healthy as each of its parts, and they will do everything they can to promote the well-being of every individual they take under their wing as employee or as customer.

REPLACING MYTHS WITH FACTS

Myth: Being Gay Is a Choice

Fact: Being gay is not a choice any more than being straight is a choice. Being gay is the same as being left-handed versus right-handed or being blue-eyed versus brown-eyed. No choice is involved in any of these characteristics.

Myth: Gays Don't Want to Mix with Other People

Fact: Gay people are human, and humans are social animals. All people, as individuals, have their own style. Some are very social and prefer to work in groups; others prefer to work alone. Whether a person is gay or straight has nothing to do with how she or he prefers to socialize, but it is obviously easier for a gay person to socialize in a safe environment than in one that is or can become hostile.

Myth: Homosexuality, Bisexuality, and Asexuality Are Mental Illnesses

Fact: Nonheterosexuality is not a mental illness. The American Psychiatric Association removed homosexuality from the *Diagnostic and Statistical Manual of Mental Disorders* close to thirty years ago. In 1999, the American Psychiatric Association, the American Psychological Association, and the psychoanalysts group within them dropped any ideas or endorsement of any idea or method to try to "cure" nonheterosexuality and, furthermore, dropped any restrictions on people of a nonheterosexual orientation in their own training programs. These associations also declared in 1999 that homophobia, not homosexuality, is the real illness that people suffer from and that states should not interfere with civil marriages between gay people.

Also in 1999, a group called the Just the Facts Coalition comprising members from the American Academy of Pediatrics, the National Education Association, the American Psychological Association, and seven other groups mailed a twelve-page booklet to the heads of all the 14,700 public school districts in the nation, debunking the idea that homosexuality can be cured or that it should be cured.[4]

Myth: Gay, Lesbian, and Transgender People Want Special Rights Under the Law

Fact: According to the NGLTF (National Gay and Lesbian Task Force) in 2002, 42 percent of Americans believe that federal law prohibits discrimination on the basis of sexual orientation in the United States. All of these people are misinformed. There are no provisions for sexual orientation in the Constitution, the Americans with Disabilities Act, the Pregnancy Discrimination Act, the Age Discrimination Act, or the Civil Rights Bills of 1964 and 1972.

The equal protection clause of the U.S. Constitution is intended to protect all citizens, but some groups fall into what are known as "suspect classes." The suspect classes recognized today are differentiated by race, national ancestry, and ethnic origin. It is this lack of specified protection that makes it perfectly legal in the majority of the United States for people, usually nonheterosexual people, to be refused employment, refused a public accommodation, denied housing, or have their children taken away simply on the basis of their real or perceived orientation. It is also this lack of protection that makes it legal for nonheterosexuals to be witch-hunted from military service and for legislatures to perceive a legal basis on which to pass obnoxious laws such as the Defense of Marriage Act (DOMA). It is the interpretation of many, specifically legislators and courts in California and

Massachusetts in February 2004, that blocking same-sex marriage is in direct violation of state and federal constitutional equal protection provisions. So even though gay and lesbian people are not specifically accounted for in suspect classes, this interpretation led to same-sex marriages being performed in those (and other) places in early 2004. As I write this book, I don't know what the final outcome of these arguments will be, but I do know what the arguments are based upon, and that is equal protection provisions, the enumerated rights of Congress, and the full faith and credit of the U.S. Constitution.

As of January 2005, fourteen states provide full legal protection to all their citizens for the purposes of employment, housing, credit, and public accommodations (Hawaii, California, Nevada, Wisconsin, Minnesota, Vermont, Connecticut, New Jersey, Massachusetts, New Hampshire, Rhode Island, Maryland, New York, and New Mexico). Another twenty or so states and about 400 other jurisdictions within states have executive orders or ordinances (these carry much less than the weight of law) that provide some level of protection, usually limited to employment, on the basis of sexual orientation.

Of the fourteen states providing full legal protection, there are currently four that offer some protections (housing and employment) to citizens based on elements of gender expression (Minnesota, Rhode Island, California, and New Mexico). Four other states (Florida, New York, Oregon, and Washington) offer administrative, precedent, or status as a disabled person protection to persons with a nonconforming gender. About seventy-one local jurisdictions provide some protections to persons for the purposes of employment regarding gender-identity expression, and several hundred jurisdictions provide some protections to citizens based on sexual orientation through executive orders or ordinances.

All state laws relative to sexual orientation specifically exempt insurance and benefits, but two of the fourteen, California and Vermont (where same-sex partners can also attain civil union status affording them most, but not all, the rights/responsibilities of married couples in these states but which are not recognized by the federal government), also offer benefits to state workers and their partners regardless of sexual orientation, gender, and/or marital status. In California, the law was expanded in 2003 to allow partners to

- make medical treatment decisions on behalf of a partner who can't;
- use sick leave to care for a child, stepchild, parent, domestic partner, or child of the partner;
- adopt the child of a domestic partner using existing procedures for stepchild adoption;
- receive the same state tax exemption for health care costs that is provided to spouses/dependents;
- sue for infliction of emotional distress and wrongful death if a domestic partner is killed due to negligence;
- receive unemployment benefits if a partner is transferred by his or her company to a location not commutable; and
- file disability benefits on behalf of an incapacitated partner.

There are two very important things to remember about the facts, laws, orders, or practices in place as they affect sexual orientation in the workplace. First, legal same-sex marriage status will affect some civil rights/responsibilities that are tied to employment status. Second, any law, rule, policy, order, and so on that specifies sexual orientation pertains to all people, not just gay people. Remember, we all have a sexual orientation.

Myth: Gays Are Economically and Educationally Elite and Therefore Don't Need or Deserve Special Treatment

Fact: Gay people are in no way economically and/or educationally elite when compared to straight people, and this argument bears an extremely uncomfortable similarity to fascist and Nazi statements about Jews in the 1930s.

Gay people are not smarter than their straight counterparts, and no institution in the country has affirmative action based on nonmajority sexual orientation. This bias about gays being intellectually superior derives from the fact that for many years, the only way for researchers or marketers to get information from "the gay community" was to send out questionnaires to people who subscribed to magazines such as *Echelon* or *The Advocate*. The fact is that people who subscribe to magazines—any people and any magazines—are people who have the time, the money, and the intellectual interest to want to read them. Therefore, people who subscribe to magazines, everything from

Newsweek to *Field & Stream,* are typically in a higher income bracket and have completed more years of formal education. Whether this makes them either economically or intellectually elite is seriously questionable.

Myth: Gays Should Not Work with Children Under Any Circumstances

Fact: Absolutely no evidence suggests that gay people should not work with, advise, counsel, or parent children. All evidence is to the contrary. Gays do not "recruit" and they do not have a secret, pervasive desire to molest children. The first concept is nothing short of silly, since you cannot "recruit" into a sexual orientation; and the second is so irresponsible that it warrants no further comment except this: More than 90 percent of sexual abuse and child molestation is perpetrated against children (typically girls) by heterosexual adult males who are usually members of their own families or who are known to them.[5] Pedophilia is a psychosis and pedophiles need serious help.

Women, especially gay women, almost never sexually molest children, and data also suggest that many men who victimize young boys do not self-identify as gay. In fact, many male abusers of boys are married, with long heterosexual histories.[6]

Myth: If A Gay Person Comes Out to Me and I Don't Approve, I Have to Pretend That I Do

Fact: If a person tells you that she or he is gay, you should respond honestly. If that means you are able to be supportive of her or his efforts at work or otherwise, even though you don't approve of this aspect of her or his personal life, you should feel free to say that. If it is *homosexual sexual behavior* that is problematic for you, you should have no qualms about expressing that opinion in an appropriate way. A great deal of progress can be made if people pay more attention to the fact that although they may have a problem with sex as a verb (regardless of who's doing it) in much the same way that they have a problem with violent behavior, it is the behavior they object to, not the person.

So if you wish to express your disapproval of certain behaviors, it is well within your rights to do so. But you should endeavor to remember that this opinion does not mitigate in the least your responsibility to allow others to be who they are, free from discrimination and irrational hatred. And if you work in human resources (HR) or diversity or in organizational development (OD) or educational services at an organization and you have opinions that make it difficult for you to provide equal attention or service or inclusion to persons based on sexual orientation, you should know that you are entitled to those opinions, but you should consider getting another type of position. It is your responsibility to be able to learn enough about sexual orientation and gender identity so as to be able to balance your professional responsibilities with your personal beliefs. If your personal beliefs honestly keep you from being able to do your job equitably for everyone affected by it, then you need to get another job.

Myth: I Can Always Tell if a Person Is Gay

Fact: No distinguishing characteristics of gay people set them apart physically, emotionally, intellectually, or spiritually from straight people. There is no skin color, no hairstyle, no eye color, no fashion, lifestyle indicator, mannerism, or anything else that identifies a person as gay or straight. You cannot tell whether a person is gay just by looking at her or him. The only way to know for sure is to ask.

Similarly, you cannot accurately judge a person's potential behavior or abilities by his or her sexual orientation once known. Sexual orientation has nothing at all to do with a person's ability to teach, to police, to soldier, to construct, to mop up, to play football, to dance, to write, or to do anything else.

Myth: If My Organization Supports Inclusion of Sexual Orientation in Workplace Diversity Programs, It Will Pay a Negative Price in the Market and in Public Opinion

Fact: No evidence suggests that being supportive of sexual orientation in workplace programs, whether in the form of nondiscrimination policies, educational initiatives, or benefits policies, results in loss of market share or revenues for the organization. In fact, overwhelming evidence suggests that the opposite is true. Please refer to Chapter 1 for some specific statistics related to inclusion and its effects in the marketplace.

Chapter 4

Meaningful and Effective Workplace Sexual Orientation Education

In Chapter 3 I discussed why it was imperative to understand what the terms *sexual orientation* and *homophobia* do and do not mean. Certainly, imparting this understanding to people who participate in my education programs is a huge focus of my work, and in this chapter I explain exactly how that is accomplished.

Before diving into all that, there's another reason why understanding where a person is coming from is paramount to having success when trying to teach. You have to meet people where they are, not where you want them to be. I cannot be an effective teacher if I expect people to just "get it" or if I assume I know where they are on these topics because they are Southerners, or Midwesterners; or that they served in Vietnam or Korea; or that they are blue-collar versus white-collar workers. I have to take some time to try to find out where each person I interact with is on the subject at hand in order to say or show him or her something that will affect him or her right there in that very spot.

In terms of education in the workplace, there are really only two ways to do this. One is to do a formal assessment, either in person or remotely/electronically; the other is to talk to people. I'll get to the former in a moment, but I'd like to say something about the latter now.

I start many of my programs and presentations, as I did the first two editions of this book, talking about being left-handed when people just assume that I am talking about being gay or lesbian. I talk about the inherency of some human characteristics, the percentage of the population that share the characteristic, and the way people with this trait have throughout history been subject to prejudice, humiliation, discrimination, and negative preconceptions never substantiated by fact. I go on to point out how the very words used to describe us in just about every language are derogatory in nature and in origin, and how religion and superstition have forever derided people with this characteristic, blaming them for everything from natural disasters to diseases and just about every shortcoming ever known to humankind. And then, of course, I go on to communicate that I am referring to a left-handed person, not a gay person.

It's a friendly way to break the ever-present ice at every program or presentation that I do, because people seem to enjoy the gentle deception as well as all the fun facts I share about how left-handed people really have suffered indignations of many kinds for centuries. No one fails to see the correlation I'm trying to make between handedness and orientation, and most people seem to respond to it in the same good-natured way that it's offered.

But it's more than just an icebreaker and over the years has come to demonstrate to me, as a facilitator, the importance of knowing where my participants in every workplace are starting from on the subject of sexual orientation.

The fact is that, in general percentages, the picture of handedness and sexual orientation looks something like this:

Right-handed	80 percent	Heterosexual
Left-handed	10-15 percent	Homosexual
Ambidextrous	2-3 percent	Bisexual
Ambidextrous	1-2 percent	Asexual[1]

What I've learned over the years is that for a lot of people it comes down to nothing more than this: There are undoubtedly more heterosexual people in the world, so being straight is indisputably normal. Just as in Leviticus, where left-handedness is singled out as a blemish that a priest cannot have, nonheterosexuality has been labeled an imperfection in a human being. The parallels to how left-handed people were and in some cases still are treated terribly by a right-handed world and how gay people are similarly treated horribly in a straight world are many. But beyond those, it is important for me or anyone else who wishes to teach and effect positive change in people's behavior in the workplace to know where our students are starting from. Where many I've met are starting from is simply that there are more straight people, therefore being straight is right and anything else is wrong. Knowing this is incredibly powerful and important for me as an instructor because from here I can accurately assess the type and bias of homophobia that I may encounter in the people with whom I work. Then, if I can explain my observations to them about what I'm hearing them say, it sometimes all by itself engenders the type of behavioral change the organization is seeking.

I don't think anything under the sun is more effective or important than the continued education and growth of people, no matter how old they are. In this chapter, we'll take a detailed look first at the elements of a solid education process and then at what the content should comprise.

DIVERSITY EDUCATION MUST BE A PROCESS

Adults rate corporate-sponsored education programs higher for reliability than any other information source. More than half of the adult employees surveyed would like more workplace education that delivers information about what they consider to be difficult issues.[2] The New York Business Group on Health learned this when they were building the first-ever HIV/AIDS education program for adults in the workplace. What it means to those of us addressing or sponsoring tough topics in diversity training is that we start every program with a generous amount of interest and goodwill from our participants. It's vitally important to leverage this interest by making sure that the program will be effective in that environment and viewed as part of a whole strategy of information dissemination and not just a knee-jerk response to the cause du jour. In other words, the process is not about developing a finite initiative; it's about developing a sense of never-ending possibilities. This process has four steps:

Step 1: Commit to an open-ended, open-minded process of workplace education.

Step 2: Apply a needs-assessment tool to evaluate the environment of the organization concerning sexual orientation.

Step 3: Actually use the data collected by the assessments to develop the course.

Step 4: Be willing to constantly evaluate and update your materials.

Step 1: Commit to an Open-Ended, Open-Minded Process of Workplace Education

Without the committed and full support from appropriate management, up to and including the highest echelons of an organization, the process will not only fail, it will never get started. The experience of the diversity manager at a petroleum company, who could speak about sexual orientation only anonymously, attests to this:

> I hope to address sexual orientation at work in our diversity education, but my organization is not willing to deal with this part of diversity in public. Sexual orientation is still that one area of diversity that makes them say, "Well, I'm not going to discriminate against them because they are gay, but I'm not going to value the fact that they are gay either" and of course, that attitude and stance results in discrimination.

> We don't have a lot of latitude over what we do at our site. I know we have gay people here who are suffering and that their suffering has a negative impact on our bottom line, but when I told our headquarters group that we wanted to include gay issues, there was no inclination to commit to that education. So all I know is, if I don't get support from our diversity management group, I won't be able to do anything.

Step 2: Apply a Needs-Assessment Tool to Evaluate the Environment of the Organization Concerning Sexual Orientation

Tweaking organizational thinking to accept education as part of a diversity process—and to include sexual orientation as part of that education—is most easily accomplished by doing a needs assessment. Some call it a "cultural audit" or "cultural evaluation." Needs assessments have a clear relationship to a common management principle: No solution will be applied to any problem or potential problem until management is sure a problem exists.

Go back to the beginning of any honest diversity effort and you'll find without exception that it started with an assessment of the environment. Whether the assessment is undertaken because human resources management takes the initiative, or whether it is an action forced on the organization by the activism of a group of employees (which is common in the case of sexual orientation), these assessments are vital to the development of a solid diversity effort. For non-heterosexual, nontraditionally gender-identified people in the workplace, these assessments can also be the first time management acknowledges their existence at all.

There's a catch, of course. The catch is that many organizations won't ask questions remotely involving sexual orientation or gender identity on the grounds that it is "illegal" or "an invasion of privacy" to do so. The truth is, they are just uncomfortable and so they don't do it. There's nothing illegal about asking questions based on one's sexual orientation because, as we've seen in previous chapters, sexual orientation is not covered in any current federal law or act, and in the fourteen states and various jurisdictions that do provide for it in aspects of workplace protection, the whole idea is to help avoid discriminatory treatment. People who object to doing assessments, fearing some always-nebulous, never-specified illegality are confusing thinking around EEO policy (i.e., disparate treatment of an included class of people) with reality. Asking questions about sexual orientation and/or gender identity does not create disparate treatment of a legally defined and protected class, because gay and transgender people are not classified as such.

Again, asking about the work environment relative to one's orientation means you are asking everyone—straight, gay, bisexual, or asexual—what they think. If you don't ask people what they think, how are you going to find out?

If people feel as though they can't stand up, come out, and make their needs known, then their needs most likely won't be addressed. On the other hand, if a fear of coming out of the closet exists around sexual orientation and/or gender identity, this should be a solid indication to management that a problem exists in the first place.

Take, for example, a statistic that comes from the Ford Motor Company: Only ten percent of the membership in Ford GLOBE (Gay, Lesbian or Bisexual Employees) comes from production plant/ manufacturing facilities, but 90 percent of the reported instances of the harassment of gay workers comes from those facilities. What this means is that while gay people in those environments are still unsure whether to or are downright afraid to come out of the closet at work, they are being victimized on the basis of their sexual orientation. So when Ford took steps a few years ago to introduce diversity education inclusive of sexual orientation, they went to great lengths to make sure it was available in their plants. They would not have known to do that unless they had asked.

Assessments can be done in facilitated focus groups, where a group of people, and maybe a series of groups, are asked to fill out the assessments and then participate (if they wish) in a live debriefing of the tool. No names are used and, depending on the organization, pains are taken to bring people in from different parts of the operation who typically don't work together or know each other. This is to ensure that people will feel free to be honest and hopefully will know that their comments will be kept strictly anonymous and confidential.

Another way to do assessments, thanks to technology, is to distribute them to a targeted group of people, perhaps members of the sexual orientation/gender identity employee network if there is one, and/or to management at a certain level, and/or to HR people in various parts of the organization. Using technology to do these assessments also makes it much easier to ask questions of one group that might not be appropriate to another. For example, managers will have a different perspective on interpersonal relationships in their groups than the HR reps probably will, and things of that nature. Again, anonymity is strictly protected, and technology makes the distribution and collection of data inexpensive and time effective.

A third method, and one that I employ frequently, is for the curriculum developer/facilitator to do one-on-one interviews of key personnel in the site or sites where the education program will be rolled out. This is typically done by a trained, professional diversity consultant, and it is typically not anonymous, although the anonymity of the respondent is somewhat protected by the fact that the facilitator is usually an outsider who won't be sharing the information gathered except for purposes of laying out the environment regarding sexual orientation to management and/or developing an education program.

The bottom line is, there are three points in collecting data. First, find out the potential or existing trouble spots about which the organization can do something. Second, use the information culled to construct an educational program leading to a safe, productive workplace for everyone. Third, help reinforce the idea that education is part of a diversity management effort, not an initiative aimed at valuing diversity. They are not the same. Diversity management looks at and tries to improve corporate culture for the sake of productivity and profitability. Valuing difference is directed at changing personal bias. When it comes to sexual orientation education in the workplace, changing behavior is the key. If biases are changed, it's a bonus.

In Appendix III, I've provided some examples of the interrogatories I've used in assessment tools over the years.

Step 3: Actually Use the Data Collected by the Assessments to Develop the Course

There are no quick fixes or easy answers to questions that concern any part of being human, and these days this may be more true of sexual orientation and gender identity than of any other aspect of employee diversity. Therefore, it is incumbent on the course developer(s) to come up with a few variations of the intended course content and then to have the opportunity to take each out for at least one spin, preferably more. This is what I call the piloting part of education program implementation, and I present more detail about it when discussing the specific elements of implementation, of which piloting is but one.

Of course, any talk of using data to develop curriculum is also speaking to specific aspects of content. Content is discussed in great detail in the next section. Suffice it to say for now that the content used and piloted must be a reflection of what is learned from the assessment.

Step 4: Be Willing to Constantly Evaluate and Update Your Materials

Reinforcement has two parts: accountability and regular reevaluation. Accountability is determined in two ways. First is whether education about sexual orientation is perceived as fully integrated in the overall strategy of the organization. Second is whether the organization identifies a person or persons who are held directly responsible for making sure that initiatives are enforced.

A focal point is necessary for a program on a topic that has the potential to cause some consternation among members of the workforce. Typically I've found that the consternation happens more before a program is actually offered than after one; people think that a course of education on sexual orientation will be much different than it actually is. It's also been my experience that even the most adamant naysayers get something out of a well-designed course and, at the very least, have no reason to fear what transpires during it.

Making a single person at each site accountable for the course at that site is very important so that people with opinions about the program, pro or con, have a knowledgeable person on site to whom they can direct their comments. This person must be empowered, or have resources available to him or her, to expeditiously respond to the comments.

Regular reevaluation piggybacks off of the accountability efforts. Every session of the program must end with an evaluation form, and every evaluation form must be read by the course designers, the facilitators, and the people responsible for the educational initiative at that site and for the organization as a whole. Diversity program facilitators who think they know everything, even about their own subject area, are bad educators. To ignore the input from a well-designed evaluation form is as bad as, or maybe worse than, ignoring the input from a predevelopment assessment. It's also unprofessional, irresponsible, and bad education.*

THREE QUESTIONS

There are three questions common to my work that are asked by almost all of my clients sooner or later:

Q: How Does the Organization Ensure That the Education Effort Won't Do More Harm Than Good?

A: I don't believe that education in and of itself ever poses a danger to anyone. However, delivered by the wrong people for the wrong

---

*A good evaluation form is one that specifically reflects the content of that particular course and how it compares to other courses the person may have taken at that workplace. It will also leave ample space for people to write comments. Also, it should never be forgotten that the data collected via evaluation, like that collected during predevelopment assessment, are places where participants should be able to note the kinds of programs or displays that they'd like to see or additional information or resources they'd like to have about the subject at hand.

reasons and without adequate preparation, education can be devastating to an organization.

One diversity director I know who requested anonymity learned this lesson the hard way. A particular employee in her company who happened to be gay was also disliked by a number of his colleagues. Being gay was acknowledged as one of the reasons he was disliked, but it was not the only reason. Being gay was, however, the aspect of this individual targeted by those who did not like him. Their gay-bashing and harassment were blatantly discriminatory and obnoxious, both to the employee and to management.

Acting in good faith, appropriate company representatives first spoke to each of the harassing employees individually and told them that their continued abuse of the individual for any reason would not be tolerated. Then management attempted to clear the air by sitting all the parties down and allowing them to express themselves. This turned out to be a very big mistake. The director told me, "In trying to educate these employees in this situation, we actually made things worse because we allowed people to express themselves and a lot of what they had to say could only be described as vehemently interpersonally homophobic. We were not prepared to address their vitriol in any constructive way at that time, and the employee who was being harassed suffered further by finding out how pointed and hateful the attitudes of his co-workers were about him."

Q: Does the Facilitator of Sexual Orientation Education Have to Be Gay?

A: No, absolutely not. Education on the topic of sexual orientation is about just that: sexual orientation, and everyone has one. The most important characteristic of a facilitator is not nonheterosexuality; it's knowledgeability and preparedness to teach the subject. I'll get to a bit more about how to train trainers who are not professional facilitators later in this chapter.

Some of the most effective facilitation I've witnessed of programs that I've helped to develop was done by heterosexual facilitators. The reason these people were so effective was that they worked hard to find examples of synchronicity between experiences in their lives and what they were trying to get people to relate to around sexual orientation. Sometimes, what really makes heterosexual facilitators so effective is that the majority of their participants are also heterosexual and are usually positively affected by hearing the information from someone they perceive to be "just like me."

However, nonheterosexual facilitators are also effective because of their ability to put a face on the issue and make it human. As we'll see when I discuss training trainers, teaming up people of different orientations to deliver this training can sometimes be the best strategy of all.

Q: Should Sexual Orientation Education Be Mandatory?

A: As I reported in the first edition, Rynes and Rosen in their study of workplace diversity education concluded that it should be mandatory for all.[3] I respectfully disagreed in the second edition of this book, and I still do. My firm opinion is that these programs should be mandatory for senior management (however that term is defined by the organization) because these are people with an obligation to make sure that they focus on behavior, not beliefs, in the workplace, but that they should not be mandatory—although freely recommended and attendance encouraged and certainly not blocked—for everyone else. I've seen with my own eyes in the past ten years that this position strongly supports the data collected by the New York Business Group on Health about what adults in the workplace value. It's also strongly supported by the reality I've seen time and again that if you build education programs well, people will come.

IMPLEMENTATION OF SEXUAL ORIENTATION EDUCATION IN THE WORKPLACE

An implementation scheme will, in overview, consist of the following elements:

- Buy in from senior management
- Piloting
- Rollout

Buy In

The process begins with sharing the data culled from the assessment with senior management and showing them, with respect for both their time and their typical desire for getting to the point, what the resultant education program will look like. My experience has been that the best results for getting senior management buy in come when they are presented with the content targeted for their organization and the general scope of the delivery plan on a long-term basis. It's extremely important that these people

- increase their awareness level about the subject of sexual orientation in their workplace so that they can make decisions about it and
- have an opportunity, in a comfortable surrounding with their peers, to discuss their own feelings and get their own questions answered so that they can behave in concert with their professional responsibilities while leaving their beliefs intact.

To fulfill these goals, I usually design a program that is more presentation, less workshop (although I do leave some exercise elements in it when I can) in conjunction with the implementers at the organization (i.e., those people who are typically charged with curriculum design and those people who usually bring such matters to light to senior management).

If the job is done correctly, the design/implementation team leaves with a mandate to develop a program for general dissemination to the organization and instructions to map out exactly what the program will look like, how long it will take, and what it will cost. Usually a member of senior management is tasked with keeping tabs on the roll out over the ensuing weeks, months, and years. Tacit approval is typically given to those who have oversight for the programs so that they can proceed in whatever manner they think best.

This last issue is very important. It speaks to the accountability factor that we previously discussed. There must be a member of senior management who is charged with knowing what's going on with this program. He or she must be kept informed via status reports, get copies of all of the evaluations from every session of the course that's offered, and have some visible way for employees to communicate with him or her about it if lower echelons of feedback cannot adequately address a question or a concern.

Piloting

Piloting of the program should be as extensive as possible and calls into play the constant reevaluation of the course prior to the generation of final materials (which really never are final).

If the organization has, for example, six levels of management that operate in four distinct kinds of facilities in every geographic region of the United States/Canada, then every attempt should be made to pilot the course to as many different combinations of these as possible. The curriculum should be drawn from elements decided upon based on the results of the assessment, and lengths of programs should be tried with different types of participant groups. I have not rolled out a long-term program based on anything less than three pilots and would not recommend it.

Of course, the people who undergo the pilot phase are not just guinea pigs for the process; they also get the benefit of the education. I also highly recommend that pilots go to what I call "worst-first" facilities. In other words, if the organization has had one or more incidents related to sexual orientation at a particular facility, pilot the program there at least once. This accomplishes two goals. First, it sends a message that the organization acknowledges that a challenge exists, and that it intends to face it head on and try to resolve it. Second, the feedback engendered from such locations is extremely valuable because you get a sense of the extremes at work in your organization. Don't shy away from these places; go there first and learn. What you learn will help build a better course faster.

Once finished with the pilot process, you may find it advisable to go back, especially to the "worst-first" sites, and offer the finished course again. Encourage people who attended the pilot to come back. They will see that their input has been incorporated, which will send another positive message that the organization is listening and acting upon what it hears.

Beyond addressing the "hot spots" in terms of place, the piloting process allows you to address the hot spots in terms of content. I cannot count the number of managers, directors, and higher persons in HR who would rather not deal with this topic because it is perceived as too tough to tackle. It is tough, but it is not impossible, and it is completely worthwhile.

Another benefit to extensive piloting is identifying people in the organization who, down the road, might make good facilitators of the program. It has been my experience that the piloting of the program, because it is so focused on feedback and getting people to think about what they are learning, causes many to fully incorporate the materials in ways that encourage their interest to want to teach it. It's good to meet these people face to face, to evaluate their reasons and their interest in facilitating the course as you are evaluating the course as a whole. When you're ready for full rollout and perhaps a train-the-educator aspect, what you've learned about some people will prove as valuable as what you've learned about the material.

Rollout

In this phase the true meaning of commitment is defined for the organization. It's here that you learn whether you're in for the long haul. Rollout plans must call for the most efficient and cost-effective ways to make the education as available as possible to the broadest number of employees conceivable. A typical model will have these elements:

- A definition of "management" for that organization across functions, facilities, and geographies. These people typically will participate in sessions of the program facilitated by a professional who had a hand in the development and design of the program.
- In conjunction with the hands-on education of management will be the identification of appropriate, suitable, qualified, interested members of the employee population who can deliver the program after receiving extensive training on how to do it. These people may be from HR, from diversity, from the employee networks, from OD, or, as noted previously, who have made themselves known during the piloting of the program.
- A number of people will be selected to undergo a "boot camp" of sorts to prepare them to teach the course. I recommend that:
  —At least twice the number of people projected to be necessary to facilitate the course to X number of people over Y time period be invited, because some of them won't come

and some of them will be dropped. This attrition rate is generally half of the original pool due either to the professional facilitator finding the person is not suited to teach the course or the individual coming to that conclusion on his or her own. This is not unusual; sometimes these courses look easier to learn and teach than they really are.

—The educators are trained to work in teams. There is a lot to know; these people generally are not professional facilitators (some are) and typically are not experts on the subject of sexual orientation (although they'll be close after the boot camp). Working in teams of two seems to be the best model, and pairing a heterosexual trainer with a nonheterosexual or nontraditionally gender-identified trainer is enormously effective in providing a balanced view of the material, especially if, as we'll discuss in the content section, using personal stories is part of the chosen curriculum.

—The boot camp should be, best case, no less than four full working days.

Once the educators have been trained, they begin to facilitate the course to participant groups of management, supervisors, salaried workers, union workers, line employees, and mixtures thereof with the professional facilitator. I recommend that the professional facilitator be present for at least the first two sessions of each team. After that, the team should be ready and able to deliver the programs themselves with or without the professional facilitator there.

Depending on size, organizations sometimes prefer that the entire rollout be handled and delivered by a professional facilitator, but I've seen no reason why excellent programs cannot be delivered by trained staff at an organization, *especially* in those cases in which the trained educators are, by profession, facilitators of workplace education.

Quite a commitment of time, energy, money, and resources is implied by this plan. However, the results of such effort, in dollars, commonly work out to be less than $100 per employee undergoing a half-day program, when these programs are offered, as per the model described here, to 2,500 to 5,000 employees over an eighteen-month period. The longer you allow the program to continue, the more people are exposed to the education at an even lower per-person cost.

Course Construction

I am a proponent of taking a modular approach to this education so that parts of what I call a "curriculum tool kit" can be mixed and matched as appropriate to the organization, based on the results of whatever assessment method I've used to determine their content need.

The course typically takes three constructs: a classic half-day training of 3.5 hours of content in a 4-hour space, 4.5 hours in a 6-hour space, or 6.5 hours in an 8-hour day. Obviously, the longer the content time, the more you can cover, but it usually means that you are able to include more participatory exercises in the flow of the course.

Modularity in development and delivery also aids an organization's efforts to put a committed, open-ended, and open-minded face on its sexual orientation education. Regardless of how well the needs assessment prepares the organization and the facilitators, new insights and unforeseen events always can instantaneously put a new spin on the whole process. Modularity allows seamless adjustment to such bumps and twists. It also allows for more content to be added over time and for present content to be continually adjusted to ensure the very best program for that organization.

Content

The bullets that follow describe some of the content pieces I draw from in order to build a class around sexual orientation in the workplace. Gender-identity content is mentioned here but is covered in much more depth in Chapter 5.

- Introductory material: An icebreaker is typically called for and there are many that can be used besides the handedness example. This is also the time to cover who the facilitators are and why they are qualified to deliver the course, as well as to present the agenda for the program. Introductory comments also typically include the business case or organizational objectives for the material, and these might in turn touch on the points of behavior that were covered in Chapter 2. In senior-management-level programs, it is often a good idea to also have the participants introduce themselves and, if they wish, mention any specific questions or concerns they have about the program they're about to participate in. Another option is to get those comments in advance and then review them without saying who in the room brought up what. In programs for people at levels below senior management, which are typically longer, there are exercises specifically designed to draw out this information.

- An example of one of these exercises is "Getting Personal." I think that a primary block to people fully engaging in sexual orientation discussions in the workplace is that they really don't understand what it has to do with being at work. This is a big disconnect caused by viewing sexual orientation as code for gay people, and also anything related to gay people being strictly about sexual activity. So the point of this exercise is to demonstrate how our sexual orientation, regardless of what it is, is something that is immediately apparent to most people, especially heterosexuality, and that none of us ever checks it at the door. We demonstrate evidence of it in just about everything we do or say, whether we realize it or not. The exercise goes on to prove that sometimes when a person doesn't share personal information it can have a disastrous effect on teamwork.

- Another exercise that can be very effective in helping people understand the intrinsic importance of sexual orientation as a part of who we are and not of what we do is a version of the "Diversity Wheel," sometimes called "Dimensions of Diversity," which draws distinctions between ways we self-identify that are inherent to us and ways we self-identify that we have chosen. Both of these exercises give participants the opportunity to introduce themselves to others and also raise issues about sexual orientation that the facilitator can pick up on and try to incorporate into the class as it goes along.

- Another important content piece is a section that breaks down sexual orientation and gender identity as part of what I call the ladder of human sexuality. The rungs on this ladder are biological sex, gender identity, gender role, sexual orientation, and sexual orientation identity. I never leave this content piece out of any course I do because it is all about what most people don't know about sexual orientation. They don't know, really, what it is. By the time this piece is over, they will know what it is, although they usually will still have questions about how these things are related but still operate independently of one another. Their residual confusion usually stems from that nagging insistence that most people are straight, so being straight is normal and everything else, while having some sort of explanation, are aberrations. The reason why this content is so powerful is that it gives people real language skills that they can use to go ahead and discuss these issues with others or simply think about them for themselves with more confidence. It's been my experience that when you give people good information and the time to process it, they usually do.

- Science and nature is an element of this education that proactively brings up issues of religion and interpretative morality. This module is based on content from Daniel Helminiak's *What the Bible Really Says About Homosexuality,*[4] as well as Bruce Bagemihl's *Biological Exuberance,*[5] Kinsey's work on human sexuality,[6] a report from the American Catholic Church called "Mixed Blessings,"[7] and statements and documents from the Episcopal Church of America as well as from different Judaic organizations around the world. Also brought to bear are all of the studies available now that weren't available even three years ago pertaining to sexual orientation as an inherent characteristic not only in humans, but in all animals that sexually reproduce. Obviously, none of this is light reading for either the instructor or the participants and must be delivered with confidence and respect.

- As mentioned earlier in this chapter, sometimes is it very powerful and effective to have a heterosexual facilitator working alone or in tandem with a gay or transgender facilitator. This is really borne out when the course includes a personal story told by one or both teachers. Whether the story is a coming-out story told by a gay or transgender person or a story about why a straight person chose to be a facilitator, it never fails to be one of the most poignant, touching, and inspiring parts of any program I've ever witnessed. No matter how hardened the participant group, people seem unable not to be affected by what the facilitator is sharing, even if it's only an appreciation of how much courage it takes for someone to stand up and tell a personal tale to a room full of strangers or colleagues.

- Two examples of content are designed to help people practice the new information and language they've been exposed to in the course. One is called a "Continuum Choice" exercise; the other is a "Practical Application" exercise.
  - "Continuum Choice" is not always used, but it allows people in the class, typically during the second part of the class, to respond to a hypothetical situation in the workplace by giving not their personal opinion, but rather their opinion of where they think the organization would come down on the issue at hand. The point of this exercise is to allow people to express an opinion using terms and words that they have, hopefully, a better understanding of at this point in the class, but without having to take personal responsibility for the opinion they are espousing.
  - "Practical Application" exercises are always used in my courses and at least an hour, if not more, is allowed for them. This part of the course includes case studies that are either drawn from actual events at that organization around sexual orientation and/or gender identity, or they are drawn from the library of actual cases I've built over the years. The participants are told that all the cases are real; however, they are not necessarily told which ones occurred at that organization, and certainly no one is ever identified by name or position as having been involved. The participants work in teams to discuss the case as it's been presented to them and then to answer questions about it. They are asked to try to come to a consensus in their teams, but it's not mandatory that they do. The exercise is intended not only to help participants use new words and terms but also to see what sorts of things can—and do—occur in the workplace around these aspects of diversity. It also forces them to take a stand on the case, but in an environment where it is safe for them to do so.

Support Materials

I also put a lot of thought and emphasis into what printed materials the participants get in conjunction with the course. Typically, a participant guide is developed and distributed that presents the key points of the course, serves as a workbook for use during the program, and provides background and additional resource material for the participants to take away with them. Usually this includes the objectives for the course, the core values driving the course at that organization, the business principles driving the course at that organization, key points of course content, specific strategies participants can use to engender change in their workplace (the tools and techniques offered in Chapter 2), a bibliography that includes books representing all points of view on the topics at hand, a list of additional resources both internal and external to the organization, and, without exception, an evaluation form.

I ask all participants to take a few moments to fill out the evaluation form as completely as possible. In cases in which there is an identifiable point of accountability at that worksite, you can also offer the option of taking the form with them to think over for a couple of days, in order to provide the best feedback possible. My feeling about this is that they've just been hit with a great deal of information to process; they should be given time to process it if it's certain that the evaluations can be recovered.

Chapter 5

Meaningful Education and Policy About Gender Identity

As I mentioned in Chapter 1, the "T" in LGBT stands for transgender. In this chapter we will learn why it's not precisely correct that transgender people be lumped in with issues of sexual orientation in the workplace, because being transgender has nothing more to do with a person's sexual orientation than not being transgender does. However, there's nothing wrong with transgender people being aligned with the gay community, even though, to their discredit and my distaste, some gay people think that there is something wrong with this alignment. These are gay people who think including transgender issues in the fight for civil or workplace rights makes it more difficult for gay people to get what they believe they deserve. I find it perplexing and ridiculous that people who are fighting for inclusion can try to make it difficult for others to join in that very same fight.

It's interesting and instructive for me to remember that when Sue and I started Common Ground in 1993, we couldn't get a place on any major HR association or group's agenda for any sort of meeting or conference because they could not handle the word *gay.* Now it seems to me that sometimes people are grateful if I'm going to address only sexual orientation in the workplace and not expand the discussion to include transgender people and gender-identity issues. I guess Gilda Radner was right: it is always something.

It is the perception of most of the world that transgender people are always also gay that causes the T to be added to the LGB. According to the Center for Gender Sanity,[1] one-third of transgender people identify as heterosexual, one-third identify as homosexual, and one-third identify as bisexual. These are not precise thirds, as a very small percentage of the sample reported being asexual.

WHAT TRANSGENDER IS

Transgender is an umbrella term that includes transsexuals, intersexuals, cross-dressers, transgenderists, and androgynes. A lot has changed regarding gender-identity workplace issues since the second edition, starting with just the words associated with the various types of people we are talking about.

For example, the term *androgyne* (from *androgynous,* which means to have male and female characteristics) is new to me but seems a far better choice of word than *hermaphrodite* and certainly much better than *a he/she,* a particularly vile label that was in vogue for a surprisingly long time. In even more common use in some organizations that are proactively inclusive of gender identity and gender identity expression is the word *intersexual.* Intersexual denotes a person whose biological sex attributes may be classically male or classically female or a mixture of both, but regardless of that, whose gender identity is fluid and they are comfortable and happy with that fluidity.

By the same token, as words such as androgyne and intersexual have become more common and familiar to people, the word *transvestite* seems to have fallen decidedly out of favor. Transvestite is, or at least was, a psychiatric term for male cross-dressers who put on women's clothing for sexual excitement. My research indicated that most cross-dressers, for whom there is no sexual stimulation involved in the behavior, always preferred not to be called transvestite, and now even people who previously identified themselves as transvestite are more likely not to use the term. I am not able to say why this is, but I would hazard a guess that because transvestite was a term coined by psychiatrists, which implied that something was wrong with such a person, people don't want to do anything that associates any aspect of transgender with mental illness.

Transgender in any manifestation—from being a theatrical drag queen to being transsexual—is not a mental illness. It is a degree (either casual [cross-dresser] or profound [transsexual]) of what is now correctly referred to as gender dysphoria. Gender dysphoria is a disagreement (not a disorder) between a person's biological sex and his or her gender identity.

At this time, I think it's still true that transitioning transsexuals have the greatest impact on the workplace, so much of this chapter's content focuses on them. However, I have started to see that some organizations' stances on gender identity and gender-identity expression/inclusion are broadening the discussion to include other types of transgender people. I've no idea where this increased awareness and inclusion will lead, but it does behoove me to identify all of the people who fall under the transgender umbrella before moving along to those aspects of the part of diversity specific to transsexual people.

WHAT TRANSGENDER REFERS TO

Intersexuals and androgynes are defined in the previous section; transsexual will be defined in its own section to follow. Other words important to our discussion of gender identity in the workplace are *transgenderist* and *cross-dresser.*

Transgenderists are transsexual people who choose not to have sex-reassignment surgery. They will probably, although not necessarily, cross-live (see next section) and/or take part in hormonal therapies that would cause certain sex-characteristic changes. The degree to which they decide to transition their sex can have an impact on others in a working environment, so it's important to at least know what the word means.

Cross-dressers are people whose gender expression is sometimes at odds with their biological sex. It is a casual, or gentle, gender dysphoria. Most cross-dressers are males whose gender identity is male, and most identify as heterosexual. They dress as women on occasion and usually hope to "pass" as women. There are also female cross-dressers who, like their male counterparts, identify as their biological sex as they were born to it and report being heterosexual. No reliable information is available to explain why most cross-dressers, and most transgender people for that matter, are born with male biological sex characteristics and a gender dysphoria leaning toward a feminine identity.

Until recently, it was observed that cross-dressing is a mostly private behavior, which is to say that although a man or woman's spouse or partner might know he or she cross-dresses, probably not too many others would know about it save other cross-dressers with whom he or she interacts. There are cross-dressing associations and clubs in most major cities in the United States, and it used to be the case that if a man was a cross-dresser who lived and worked in New York, he would probably go some distance, for instance to the club meeting in Boston or Chicago, to specifically avoid an accidental meeting with a friend or colleague while cross-dressing. However, what organizations are starting to experience is the desire of cross-dressers they employ to occasionally cross-dress at work. We will discuss this a bit more when we look at the difference between a nondiscrimination policy that includes the words "gender identity" and one that includes the term "gender identity/expression."

TRANSSEXUALS

Transsexuals are people whose gender identity does not match their biological sex. It is a profound gender dysphoria that a person feels overwhelmed by and must deal with. Male-to-female transsexuals begin life with typical male biology and identify as girls and then women. Female-to-male transsexuals start out with typical female biology and identify as boys and then men. Transsexuals are motivated to transition their sex so that it matches their gender identity. Sex reassignment, although not easy or cheap, is possible. Gender-identity reassignment is impossible.

When we talk about transsexuals, most people think of male-to-female transsexuals, but it is important to recognize that there are also many female-to-male transsexuals. According to Lynn Conway in "How Frequently Does Transsexualism Occur?" as many as 200,000 people have gone through transition during the past several decades in the United States and perhaps 10,000 or more do so every year now.[2] For many reasons, transsexual men do not cause as much social concern as transsexual women. It is more acceptable in our culture for women to wear men's clothing than for men to put on dresses. In fact, most male attire has been appropriated as fashionable clothing for women, including suits, tailored shirts, and ties. Some features of women's clothing, such as shoulder pads, make them look more masculine and enhance a woman's aura of authority and competence.

However, for men to wear dresses or breast padding detracts from their credibility and their status and may be considered scandalous. What's interesting, and what we cover in an education program that discusses the ladder of human sexuality, is that what people seem to get up in arms about usually has almost nothing to do with the individual at hand. It has to do with whether or not a person lives up to cultural or societal expectations of the characteristics of "a real man" or "a real woman," which has everything to do with gender-role expectations and nothing to do with a person's sense of himself or herself as a man or a woman.

Most of the media attention, therefore, has been directed at transsexual women. As female-to-male transsexuals become more politically active, access medical care more frequently, and form social and political organizations, it may become apparent that there are roughly as many transsexual men as there are transsexual women.

The Business Case

Simply put, and as more than one transsexual person has said to me, a person undergoing sex reassignment is not having a lobotomy. Whatever that person was capable of doing before, especially intellectually and skillfully, he or she is still capable of doing. So the bottom line is that it makes sense to retain people who do a good job.

As Janis Walworth of the Center for Gender Sanity and I put it in our co-authored section of *A Trainer's Guide to Training Tough Topics,*[3] two more precise elements of the business case for being supportive and cooperative with a transitioning person include the following:

- A transitioning transsexual can be viewed similarly to a person who is permanently or temporarily disabled, who becomes pregnant, or who receives permission to observe various religious practices or holidays. Accommodations are not atypical in any of these situations.
- There are no direct cost implications to the organization unless it explicitly provides for coverage of aspects of transsexual transition in employee insurance plans. This is not common practice in the private sector, and only one or two municipalities in the United States provide this kind of economic support. Some cost implication can be found in the need for the transitioning employee to get some out-of-scope paid leave, but these leaves are not inordinately long or disruptive if discussed prior to their occurring.

Another element of the business case can be interpreted to include whether a company is legally obligated to let a transsexual person transition on the job or to help her or him. Firing a worker because she or he is transsexual can incur lawsuits, particularly in those states where laws protect workers from discrimination based on gender identity and/or expression or in which courts have interpreted state and federal sex or disability discrimination laws to protect transsexual people.[4]

NONDISCRIMINATION POLICIES

Since the matter of law has come up, it's a good time to discuss the difference between a policy that protects people in the workplace from discrimination on the basis of "gender identity" and those that specify "gender identity/expression."

As I stated in Chapter 2 when discussing nondiscrimination policies in general, such a policy is no more than a statement of good intentions. Absolutely nothing, aside from intent, makes an organization honor its own nondiscrimination policies, but it's been my experience that most of them do intend to stand behind them. The problem is, sometimes people don't know what their nondiscrimination policy says, even when they're the ones who actually wrote it.

If an organization includes the words *gender identity* in its nondiscrimination policy and does not include words such as compensation or benefits to the status, then they are saying that a person who is transsexual can expect nonharassing treatment and organizational support in the form of reasonable accommodations for his or her transition. They are not in any way promising financial aid for transition, but it is common that organizations have found a way to help with the monetary part of sex reassignment and have certainly cooperated in efforts to have the therapy and hormonal parts of treatment covered under EAP and/or prescription drug plans.

If an organization includes the phrase *gender identity/expression* in their nondiscrimination policy, then they are not only stating the intent in the immediately preceding paragraph but also that they will protect employee's rights to express their gender as the employee sees fit. So, if an employee occasionally chooses to cross-dress at work, by including the *expression* part of the phrase, the organization is saying it will support that choice.

I make no value judgments with my clients as to whether this is a viable plan. Being transgender makes perfect sense to me, but many people are still in the deep woods about it. All I tell my clients is if you are going to add the language to your nondiscrimination policy (and I urge them to do so whenever I can), know what you are adding. I have had client companies say they are afraid that allowing cross-dressing would create an unsatisfactory work environment for the cross-dresser's co-workers, and others have maintained it would be no problem if the situation were adequately explained in advance.

Education is always key. I think it's probably unfair to ask co-workers of a cross-dresser or a transsexual to "get with the program" without providing information as to what is going on with that person. There is more latitude with accepting cross-dressing than transsexualism in a workplace. A cross-dresser really does have a choice; a transsexual does not. It is vital that the organization adequately prepare itself and all its members for whatever elements of transgender diversity it plans to acknowledge and accommodate. That preparation is called a transition plan.

TRANSITION PLANNING

Standards of Care

The information I'm presenting in the section about transition planning is directed at what the organization can and should do during the stages of an individual's transition. There are transition planning elements that I've found specifically for transitioning transsexuals, and I've listed some of those excellent sources in the bibliography.

As Janis Walworth notes in her excellent paper about managing transition, no two transitions are the same for any two people who undergo them. Not only have I learned this from the always excellent information put out by the Center for Gender Sanity but it's also been driven home for me time and again by the many courageous and good-humored transsexual men and women that I've met in the past few years. One thing they have always seemed to agree on: there are standards of care and at least the semblance of a reliable process to help guide a successful transition.

The "Standards of Care for Gender Identity Disorders" that I have relied on come from the Harry Benjamin International Gender Dysphoria Association. These standards recommend a multifaceted transition specifically listed as follows:

- At least six-month evaluation with a psychotherapist is necessary before irreversible changes are undertaken.
- After six months, the psychotherapist can recommend that the transsexual begin receiving hormone treatments.
- A period of one year or more of *cross-living,* called the *real-life experience* or, these days, just *"living,"* is required before a recommendation for sex-reassignment surgery can be made. This recommendation must be made by two therapists, one of whom must have a doctorate. Cross-living is living full-time in the transsexual's new gender role, which gives the transsexual a chance to experience what life will be like after surgery. This means working or attending school, shopping, exercising, relaxing, relating to friends and family, going to church or temple, sleeping, and eating—doing everything in the new role. Through cross-living, changing sex becomes more than a theoretical idea; the realities of life as a woman or a man cannot be ignored. The transsexual is then better equipped to make a final decision about whether to continue with sex-reassignment surgery. It's a decision never made lightly because it is very difficult, or impossible, to reverse, whereas cross-living or even hormonal therapy are, to a great extent, reversible.[5]

Of course, time and money will also play a role in whether a person has sex-reassignment surgery. Currently this surgery is considered elective (if it's considered at all) and no insurance plan that I've found will cover it. The time is related to whether the transsexual person can get or afford to take the necessary time off that such surgery requires.

At one time it was quite common for transsexuals to have to quit or dramatically change their jobs, sell their houses, or otherwise move in order to start a new life. Such extreme changes were sure to pull whatever emotional or financial support they had out from under them. It was asking a person to give up every semblance of familiarity and security in her or his life at a time when familiarity and security would be paramount. Happily, in both theory and practice such an upheaval is no longer recommended or expected.

The Paperwork

According to Walworth's research, as documented in "Managing Transsexual Transition in the Workplace," coming out at work may be and often is one of the last steps in a person's transition. What this means is that, for example, a male-to-female transitioning person may have also changed her passport, driver's license, credit cards, accounts, and other documents into her new name, which she would have been able to do around the time she began hormonal treatments and/or living as her target sex. However, she may not come to work as a female until she is sure that the organization is going to be supportive. When contacted either by the transitioning employee or a trusted intermediary, the organization, typically the HR department, will have to determine with the transsexual a "start date" for her in her target sex. This will allow not only for a smooth communication strategy, including education of others within and outside of the organization who will be affected by the person's transition, but also for HR to catch up with the individual's necessary documentation changes. Paychecks, insurance policies, employment records, tax accounting, and banking arrangements will all have to be changed to reflect a sex and name change.

Communication Plan

What I have learned about successful transitions has come from people who have actually lived this process either as a transitioning transsexual or as a manager or HR representative working with such people. All of these successful plans had the following elements in common.

- Transsexual persons should be fully involved in the development of the transition plan to include everything from how their co-workers will be informed to which rest rooms they will use in what stages of transition to whether they will be personally involved in any education efforts that occur. The operative phrase here is "fully involved," and it does not mean fully responsible.

The option for how involved the person wishes to be should be discussed by appropriate HR personnel and management from the immediate supervisor all the way up the line. Transsexual people should never be made to feel they are the poster child for transition in the workplace. They're just people going through something extraordinary; they don't know everything about it just because they are transsexual; they are learning too. It is the organization's responsibility, and probably the first-line manager's and HR rep's responsibility, to drive the transition strategy.

- The manager must fully understand the organization's position on support of a transitioning person and specifically what that support entails. He or she must be empowered to work through the transition plan with the employee and to make decisions relative to it.
- The manager and the HR rep must be empowered to support other employees and answer their questions about what is transpiring in the workplace. They need to work as a team with a coordinated message about how the transition is going to be handled and supported.
- The manager must be empowered to ensure absolutely no harassment of the transitioning employee occurs with anyone she or he comes in contact with, be that other leadership, other employees, or customers or clients.

Managers and HR reps working with a transitioning person have to be able to do many things. The key to them actually being able to suceed is that they avail themselves of or are provided with education about gender identity and gender-identity dysphoria first.

Education

The degree to which people are misinformed or uninformed about transgender people is profound. Despite the fact that there have always been transgender people and more than 200,000 have transitioned in the United States since the 1950s, it is not a topic people have embraced. Therefore, whatever a workplace education program imparts about this subject is going to represent a 100 percent increase in the knowledge and understanding of the average person.

I always find it successful to treat adults like adults and just tell them what transgender means from the perspective of simply being an aspect of human sexuality. So I revert back to the ladder of human sexuality. Once I've explained precisely what biological sex and gender identity are, it's possible to explain how people might have a dysphoria or disagreement between who they know themselves to be and what they see when they look in the mirror pretransition. Understanding doesn't mean that people have to relate to this particular disagreement; it's admittedly hard to do if you are not transgender yourself. But people can typically relate to knowing something so strongly about themselves that no amount of external pressure or persuasion could ever convince them it was otherwise or that they could change. In fact, a way for people to relate to what a transgender person feels about the disagreement between what she or he sees and what she or he knows is often just to ask people if they would under any circumstances be persuaded that their gender identity does not match their biological sex. It's a connection so strong that the social scientists say that, on average, most people know their gender identity (whether one is a boy or a girl) on average between eighteen months and three years of age. What's interesting about this is that the average age of language acquisition is twenty-four months. This means that a significant percentage of people know who they are relative to their gender identity before they even have language to express it. Call it your soul; call it your essence; call it whatever you'd like. It is powerful, and most people can relate to that experience of *just knowing*.

Explaining it this way, and further explaining the varying degrees of gender-identity dysphoria (e.g., from drag to transsexual) never fails to help people understand what's going on. So the first people who have to learn this material are the manager(s) and HR personnel charged with working out and working through the transition plan with and for the transsexual employee. Once they get it, it becomes practicable to explain to others what the transsexual is going through and why the organization chooses to support her or him.

Communication Strategy

Once the necessary people are informed and feel capable of sharing what they've learned with others, it becomes a matter of who is going to tell whom what and when.

It's important to first determine who in the workplace will be primarily affected by the transsexual's decision to transition. That is, people in the same workgroup, project team, or on the same shift or assembly line. Then it must be determined who will be affected secondarily by the transition. This might include people who don't work directly with the transsexual individual but who do work in the same facility and can and do interact with her or him even sporadically or casually. It might also include customers and clients. It is important that these constituencies are identified as quickly as possible and that a plan is agreed upon in order to tell them what is going on. Waiting or equivocating once the transsexual employee has informed the organization that she or he plans to start living as her or his target sex on a certain date will only increase, unnecessarily, rumors and other types of misinformation making the rounds.

The Center for Gender Sanity makes the following recommendations about elements of communication:[6]

- Confidentiality of all information that the transsexual person shares with his or her manager and with HR must be ensured in the early stages. This is mostly for the protection of the transitioning employee so that he or she never feels rushed or under the gun relative to any aspect of his or her transition. It's also for the sake of the organization that all paperwork and all strategies for enabling a successful transition are put into place before the questions start.
- Just in case, a backup plan should be in place to deal with a premature disclosure of information that may occur accidentally. Senior management should be prepared to step in immediately to reinforce the organization's commitment to no harassment of the individual, the intention to inform all employees appropriately and completely about what is going on, and the intention to stick to the well-designed transition plan as originally intended.
- There may be a need for a public relations statement regarding the fact that the organization is working through a transition with an employee, in case the transition becomes public knowledge or the object of media attention.
- On occasion, transsexuals have given their permission to an HR rep to speak with their therapists. This may provide an additional source of information for the organization, and it might

also be helpful if all parties have questions about the transsexual person's ability to perform her or his job before, during, and after transition.

- A transsexual employee may at the beginning or at any time during his or her transition want to communicate with the organization only through a trusted intermediary. This desire should always be respected.
- If managers who will be affected by the transition are not part of the transition planning team, it may be a good idea to tell them prior to telling the employee's co-workers.

In terms of who does the telling, certainly the transitioning employee should be given the option of informing any or all of the constituencies. If she or he chooses not to be part of this process at all, or only for some of it, those wishes must be respected. An effective strategy, mentioned not only by Walworth but by numerous transsexual people I've known who were generous enough to speak to me, was for the transsexual to tell her or his co-workers in writing what she or he is going through and why. These letters are often accompanied by a note from appropriate management or HR personnel reiterating the organization's support of the transsexual and a sketch of how the transition plan and additional education and communication will be rolled out.

It is absolutely mandatory that once the communication begins, there be a single point of contact for co-workers to express their concerns or ask their questions. The person or persons chosen to fill that role must be as knowledgeable as possible and fully empowered to respond to these inquiries quickly and directly.

Challenges You Can Expect

Rest Room Use

Without a doubt the first and most lasting concern about a transsexual transitioning in a workplace—any workplace—is what rest room he or she will use once he or she starts living and/or undergoing hormonal therapy that results in an outward change of appearance. This may seem silly or immature to some, but it really isn't difficult to understand. We are not very mature as a society when it comes to any topic concerning genitalia or bodily functions of any kind, but certainly providing education as described previously can go a long way in helping people get over whatever discomfort they may feel about sharing a rest room with a transsexual person in any stage of transition. The fear that a transsexual may pose a sexual threat to another person is another expressed concern, but again, education goes a long way in explaining the difference between gender dysphoria and any kind of sexual perversion or tendency toward inappropriate sexual behavior.

Walworth makes the excellent point in her paper that although some people would prefer that a transsexual use the rest room appropriate to her or his sex before transition (e.g., if a male-to-female transition, that she use the men's room), many transsexuals never choose sex-reassignment surgery, and a person doesn't have to have sex-reassignment surgery to be a transitioned transsexual. Again, education would help clarify this for people.

Another excellent point made by Walworth and others is that not every person, transsexual or not, has genitalia that conforms to some predetermined standard of what male or female genitalia should look like. However, I've never heard of a situation or place that demanded some sort of "proof of genitalia regularity" in order to use a rest room.

Every transsexual I've met understands the reticence they face with co-workers when the topic is the rest room. All have indicated that reasonable accommodations during the time they are transitioning and their colleagues are learning about it are just fine. Although transsexual persons should never be expected to be really inconvenienced just to make others feel comfortable—for instance, they should never have to physically leave a building to use a rest room at the gas station down the street or even at the company's own facility across the parking lot—there are solutions that are quite acceptable.

One is that if an organization is housed in a very large or multi-floor building, that the transsexual person uses a rest room in another location or on another floor where she is not known as Bob or Bobbi or at all. If that's not practical, then a single-use facility as is typically available for disabled people may be the rest room used for a time. What's important is that everyone understands how this is going to work and that it will be asked of the transsexual employee for only a predetermined period in which employees are getting the information they need to make it in reality the nonissue it really always was.

Memory Inertia

When I first learned about memory inertia from Sara at Shell Oil, who has been one of my personal guides and teachers in matters transgender, I was fascinated because it just made so much sense. Truthfully, I don't know if Sara coined the term or not, but it's a great term. Memory inertia is when people can't instantly forget that Bobbi was Bob. They are supportive and they want to respect Bobbi and her need to transition, but if people have known Bobbi as Bob for a few years or many, many years, they are certainly to be forgiven if they slip up in how they refer to her either by name or pronoun.

Memory inertia is normal and is certainly not a problem unless a co-worker uses it as an excuse not to acknowledge and respect the transsexual. Management need only be watchful for situations in which people are getting the information needed to understand what is transpiring but seem to absolutely refuse to apply it. In these cases a form of covert harassment may be taking place that must be proactively stopped.

Challenge to Belief Systems

Some employees may very well be offended on religious grounds by a person's decision to transition from one sex to another. This is certainly another job for "behavior, not beliefs" as discussed in Chapter 2. People have every right to feel this way; they don't have any right to inflict discriminatory or harassing behavior or comments on another person just because they "don't believe in it," whatever "it" is. An organization must make it clear that although differences of opinion are certainly valid, opinions that result in harassment are not.

An Enthusiastic Transsexual

To her credit, and to our edification and benefit, Walworth points out that sometimes the transsexual employee can be the cause of disruption. Perhaps he is so excited about finally being able to transition that he tries to tell people about it constantly, even when they respectfully indicate they'd rather not discuss it. Or perhaps he is still mastering the art of dressing as men are expected to dress and is not meeting some spoken or unspoken dress code. Or it's possible that a transsexual person will be overly sensitive when dealing with another's memory inertia toward him, even though the intent of the co-worker to respect Betty's transition to Benjamin is sincere. In cases such as these, the HR rep or manager should not be afraid to have a private conversation with the transsexual employee, who may not be aware of what he is doing and would appreciate the feedback.

Accountability and Reevaluation

As with education, programs, and policies related to sexual orientation, there must also be accountability and the ability to constantly reevaluate the work environment where transition has, is, or will take place again. Some transsexual people report an unwillingness to proactively report harassment because they fear negative repercussions from the harassing co-worker or from others. They are not sure that HR and the organization will stand up for them, so they need to know and have it reinforced that the organization does support them in every way that it can and shows that it intends to remain true to the transition plan.

HR should not be afraid to take it upon itself to survey everyone, including the transsexual employee, on a regular basis for a year or more to ensure that there aren't any lingering problems for anyone.

Without a doubt, gender identity in the workplace manifesting itself as any of the classifications of transgender people has been, for the past three years, the biggest growth area in what people want to talk about relative to sexual orientation and gender-identity diversity. Perhaps only the debate concerning same-sex marriage (discussed in Chapter 8) will push it to second place for a while.

Don't ask, don't tell is a silly policy to apply to any group of people or any topic. The fact is that transgender people are everywhere and eventually every sizeable employer will deal with a transsexual transition in the workplace. I hope that people will embrace the possibilities presented by letting themselves learn about things previously strange to them. There is nothing strange about being transgender when it is understood in the context of human sexuality and gender dysphoria.

Chapter 6

Employee Networks:
Expanding Challenges and Roles

Employee networks of any kind allow people with similar interests or characteristics to interact with others who are like them. In the case of a group formed around sexual orientation, the existence of such a group may serve to help individuals who are gay or transgender know that they are not alone. Feeling like "the only one" is a depressing condition common to many gay workers.

As with any of the strategies detailed in this book, in order for employee networks to have a beneficial effect on individuals and the organization as a whole, there must be the buy in and support of management. Later I'll discuss how the structure of an employee network might look based on the combining of best practices that I've seen at all sorts of organizations over the past decade. However, right now it behooves me to say two things. First, employee networks formed based on sexual orientation and gender identity, if included, must also be fully inclusive of heterosexual people, and provision for this must be made in the name of the network.

For example, some networks are formed by making a word such as ANGLE or LEAGUE out of the company names and reference to gay people. I know what companies I got these from, obviously, but let's just say ANGLE is Acme Network of Gay and Lesbian Employees and LEAGUE stands for Lesbian and Gay Unified Employees (which it doesn't, thank goodness). There is nothing terribly wrong with either one except the obvious omissions implied by both names. There is absolutely no reference to bisexual or asexual people, certainly none to heterosexual people, and absolutely none to transgender people.

Even innocuous group names such as Pride Network or Rainbow People at Acme Corporation leave much to be desired, and it is definitely desire I'm referring to here. People want and need to see themselves reflected in the names and images of things that they associate with. We'll see in Chapter 7, which talks about the marketplace relative to sexual orientation, how prevalent this desire is. Similarly, when you are trying to successfully initiate and run a group that may have myriad effects on the organization you have to be as inclusive as possible and not leave out important constituencies. So although I know it's difficult because Lesbian, Gay, Bisexual, Transgender, Straight doesn't give one many vowels to work with, it's something to definitely think about putting more time and effort into. One organization I know uses an "A" for allies, which I think is very creative and descriptive. In short, what you call the network matters if you want many people from all over your organization to participate in it, even if their participation is occasional or at a single event.

The second point I wanted to make up front concerns participation, particularly that of management-level people. I've observed that often organizations or individuals within organizations who try to get these groups going seem to forget that members of management are employees too, with as much of a stake in what transpires as anyone else at the company. Truth be told, some management are actually not heterosexual either. The best way for these people to be involved in what's going on is to be involved in what's going on. A prevalent fear about "employee groups" of any kind has been, and continues to be in many places, that they will constitute a lobby or a union for their specific demands and that they would prove more divisive to and engender more conflict in a given workplace. So it's better to start off such an effort with a spirit of cooperation, and that means inviting management to cooperate.

A WINNING STRUCTURE
FOR EMPLOYEE NETWORKS

Sue and I developed a structure for successful employee networks when we wrote our first edition that has been implemented successfully at a number of organizations, large and small. This is what I recommend:

1. Identify a leadership team for the employee network. These people will likely, at first, be the ones who led the charge for the

employee network to be formed and probably have also done a lot of "underground outreach" to others in the organization. The network's leadership team will typically have four to six people on it and, thanks to technology, they don't have to be located in the same place.

2. The leadership team organizes subcommittees and appoints a person who is not on the leadership team to head up each one. These subcommittees can be in as many areas as are deemed necessary or desired. They can be for budget, for community outreach, for internal education, for internal and external policy, for cooperation with other employee groups, for marketing and assisting revenue generation, for liaison with HR, for communications, for Pride events, for growing membership activities. There can be, in short, a committee for everything the network thinks it would like to get into.

3. Each member of the leadership team is also the primary liaison between a committee (or, if necessary, more than one) and the leadership team. It's this person's job to know what the committee is doing, what it would like to do, what it needs, and so on so that he or she can present those things to the leadership team.

4. A member of senior management is appointed as a liaison or mentor for each person on the leadership team and, therefore, to a committee. The communication that the leadership team member shares with the team in general is also shared with his or her management liaison. In this way, an effective and orderly communication channel is created between all the committees and the organization as a whole.

What's really good about this structure is that it allows for maximum participation across the enterprise while also providing for maximum oversight of all activities of the network, communication of those activities, and control over who is doing what without it appearing as if "big brother" is watching.

Document from the Start

Chances are that the employee network is being started at a business whose ultimate, bottom-line objective is to make money. Whether it's a company that sells a product or service, a university, or even a not-for-profit, profit motive can never be far from your mind as you pursue even the most humanistic of endeavors—trying to help people come together over a shared aspect of human diversity. Even though some of what you hope to accomplish (see Objectives later in this chapter) may not seem to be hardwired to the business case and may even, sometimes, just be something you want to do because it's fun, never forget that for the most part, you are involved in serious business with serious people. Treat them and the process with respect, and you won't go wrong.

Part of treating the process with respect is documenting every part of what you want to accomplish as an employee network. The documentation should be made up of a mission statement, objectives for the network, and organizational and operational details. This last aspect has subparts that include resources, funding, confidentiality, and accountability, to name some but not all of what can come up. Let's look at each of these three components in more detail.

MISSION STATEMENT

The most important thing about the mission statement for the employee network is that it be consistent with the company's mission and philosophy, so do your research. Writing an ill-conceived mission statement is the easiest way for the organization to dismiss the intent of the group.

A sample might read something like this:

> The mission of our group, consistent with the stated philosophy and operating principles of this organization, is to provide a supportive environment for all employees regardless of sexual orientation and gender identity. We will work to encourage an inclusive work environment that fosters personal and professional growth in order to improve the work performance of each individual as well as to positively influence the profitability and productivity of the organization. We will devote ourselves to openness and education about issues related to sexual orientation and gender identity while respecting the rights and opinions of all employees, as dictated by our company's nondiscrimination policies.

This mission statement is a balance of the general and the specific and makes pains to include the operating principles and previously stated policies of the organization.

OBJECTIVES

The objectives for the employee network are statements of intent regarding what the group would like to accomplish. There are two ways to represent the objectives, either as general and all-encompassing with no particular time frame in mind, or as specific objectives for a specified time period.

General objectives might include the following:

- Sponsor informal brown-bag gatherings to provide information about issues related to sexual orientation and gender identity
- Enhance the organization's ability to market effectively to the LGBT marketplace
- Enable the company to become, and to be, an employer of choice for people regardless of sexual orientation and/or gender identity
- Develop a supplier diversity initiative that focuses on minority orientations and gender identities

Specific objectives to a time period might resemble the following:

I. 2004 goals and measures
   A. Goal: Identify more LGBT suppliers
      1. Measure: The number identified and brought on board by Q3
   B. Goal: Establish formal ties to other employee networks
      1. Measure: Cross-pollination of personnel on leadership teams for different employee networks
   C. Goal: Establish representation of this network in every region by the end of the year
      1. Measure: Member list, out and open, that reflects at least five people in each of our regions

I tend to favor time-period-specific objectives because they force the organization and the network to give some thought not only to what they'd like to do but whether what they'd like is practical in a given time frame. It makes people engage in more thought and planning. Of course, it's possible to have objective statements that are a mix of the general and the time specific, and that might be the best solution.

ORGANIZATIONAL AND OPERATIONAL DETAILS

These details of initiating and running an employee group cover such topics as the following:

- How meetings will occur and how often they will occur: Can the network have meetings on company time, using company facilities? This is a big question to know the answer to at the beginning of this journey.
- What resources are available in the organization and which of these will be available to the employee network? I recommend, as I said before, that whatever one group can use, all groups must have access to. Then the employee network should use every communications vehicle available to them, whether it be an intranet, electronic or print newsletters, brochures in the interoffice mail, or notices posted on electronic or in-building bulletin boards. If security or anonymity for in-house communications is a problem, you can consider asking for funding to put notices in the local papers that target the gay and transgender population. These exist in just about every metropolitan area (not all of course, but a lot more than at any time in the past).
- Make available a safe way (a voice-mail box, snail-mail box, or e-mail box) for people to reach out without having to identify themselves by name. To this end, you can also make sure that a person in management, ideally in the human resources department, supports the organization's desire to reach out—someone whose name is posted within the company and who is a "safe" person.
- If the company will provide leadership or other training to members of the employee network, probably those on the leadership team, try to get that in play as quickly as possible in order to

build the skill sets of these people so they can help others to effectively organize and communicate.

Be sure to respect your members' differing comfort levels with having their orientation or gender identification known. Efforts to make everyone feel as safe as possible in "coming out" typically are paramount to the mission of the group, but this comes to all in their own time and must be accommodated. People who are willing to work only behind the scenes for a while are still willing to work.

WHAT A GOOD EMPLOYEE NETWORK CAN ACCOMPLISH

It is not unusual for employee group representatives or management at a company to tell me that since they got "sexual orientation" and/or "gender identity" added to their nondiscrimination policy or they have won domestic partner benefits then they either have nothing to do or everyone who was involved in those two efforts has become decidedly disinterested in participating in anything else. What I usually ask them is, "Do you have a membership list for your network and, if so, do you have the open list and the secret list?" Easily nine times out of ten, the answer is in the affirmative. So I tell them this: if you have even one person in your organization who doesn't feel able to be on the list openly—be you 50 people or 50,000 strong—it is one too many and you still have plenty you can do.

Education

There is absolutely no doubt in my mind that the single best thing an organization can do to accommodate sexual orientation and gender identity in the workplace is to design, develop, and deliver—to everyone in the organization, no matter how long it takes—a program of education focused on these aspects of diversity. Of course, Chapter 4 was devoted to this subject so there's much more detail there, but a couple of points bear mentioning regarding employee networks and their role in initiating and helping to incorporate these programs.

The employee network can, and should, find out what kind of diversity education, if any, is being offered. If there is any, they should ascertain exactly what the content is concerning sexual orientation and gender identity. If there's no content about these things or a one-paragraph mention of them (neither is unusual), then helping the organization understand how they might build a class about these topics or incorporate them into the existing model is actually easier. You can start from the ground up and not have to worry about undoing anything that might be incorrect or misrepresentative in the current information being disseminated.

The way to find out what's in the course is to have many members of the network attend the course so as to get as many perspectives as possible. Once you know what the lay of the land is, you can research other options that your organization may want to include. If you treat this as a serious development program and deliver it as a polished outline of content or even just an overview of content with references to content experts whom applicable management can speak to, you will get a much better reception than just shooting an e-mail to the facilitator complaining about the lack of inclusion in the course.

Another way, directly related to education, that employee networks can get involved is to participate in Train the Trainer, should the organization choose to build a course with the help of a professional facilitator with an eye toward eventually turning it over to internal resources to update and deliver. Chapter 4 talks more about exactly how this is accomplished, but here it's just important to note that trainers can come from the employee network even though the people involved might not be skilled facilitators. A well-designed course and appropriate training for trainers can produce outstanding results.

BROWN-BAG FUNCTIONS

In addition to formal education programs on sexual orientation in the workplace that are a part of a full-blown diversity education curriculum, the organization can offer less formal brown-bag meetings or presentations about orientation and gender-identity issues at work.

We all know, of course, that the first rule of a successful meeting is to make sure that food will be served. Brown-bag meetings are, typically, lunchtime or extended lunchtime meetings, and there is nothing wrong with doing a program on sexual orientation in this way. But note the following:

- It should be more of a presentation than a workshop, although not very formal.
- It must have the same level of structure and preparation as a formal presentation even if it doesn't look or feel like one. It is a horrific mistake to put such a meeting in the hands of an unskilled or unprepared facilitator. Because of the sense of casualness about brown bags, people actually feel more free to act out and try to disrupt (if that is their focus), or to simply interrupt and try to get a debate or even just a discussion going.
- It must ensure that the goals and objectives for the meeting are as clear as they are in a workshop, and they must be laid out from the start. As with a workshop, there must be a set beginning and ending time. I recommend that people not be allowed to come and go freely but expected to stay for the whole event, so that nothing is heard out of context.
- It should have at least one member of senior management present. The event must be as sanctioned and as officially supported as a full-scale education program is perceived to be by most employees. This is sometimes difficult for people who are somewhat closeted to accept, but it's a very important first step in creating an environment that supports open dialogue, which will lead, hopefully, to an environment that feels safe to everyone all the time.

Brown bags are also a great opportunity to get a willing member of the employee network to talk about what it's like to be who she or he is at that place. So the network can comprise a sort of internal speakers' bureau made up of network members who are willing to stand up and tell their stories. These parts of brown bags never fail to make an impression on those listening. However, using network members as speakers should be done only in a structured context by people who have had adequate support and training and with a skilled facilitator ready to assist that person should questions or comments become unruly.

DEMOGRAPHIC/ENVIRONMENTAL SURVEYS

Organizations ask me all the time how they can gather information about gay and transgender people in the workplace. They don't know if they can ask questions related to sexual orientation and/or gender identity on employee surveys (they can), or if they know they can, they don't know what to ask. Appendix III of this book has some sample survey questions, and anyone can contact me to discuss what to ask, why, and how to do it, but where the employee network membership can come in is to be the guinea pigs, if you will, for an initial try at doing such a survey. If you want to know what the environment is like for gay and transgender people in your workplace, ask them. They'll be delighted you asked. If you want to ask others who don't identify as gay how they perceive the environment, you can survey heterosexual members of the employee network (if there are any) or you can ask some of your managers to take the survey and tell them why. You can also ask managers in several areas of your organization to identify people who work for them that they are relatively sure are heterosexual and not transgender if they'd agree to take the survey.

Not doing these assessments is a benign form of homophobia. It's not hateful or dangerous, but it keeps the organization from getting valuable information about itself when applying just a little creativity and energy would enable that information to be gathered.*

Mentoring and Coming-Out Coaches

Over the past decade, mentoring has established itself as an effective and respected mechanism to leverage the strengths of individuals in the workplace. The concept of mentoring is simple. A person who is already established, usually in an upper-management position, takes a specific individual (perhaps more than one) under her or his wing and personally monitors and contributes to that individual's advancement. When applied to diversity, however, mentoring takes on additional meaning.

Instead of one-to-one mentoring, I advocate that organizations explore a system of corporate mentoring in which team-to-team replaces one-to-one guidance. The idea behind corporate mentoring is

---

*A discussion regarding legal misconceptions about assessments that cover sexual orientation and gender identity is in Chapter 4.

that it brings qualified individuals, regardless of race, gender, orientation, or what have you, into the executive level by extending the concept to whole groups instead of just individuals. This is a merit system rather than a predictive one.

In a predictive mentoring system (one to one), certain assumptions are made about the person's ability. In corporate mentoring, there are no subjective predictions; there is only performance. The responsibility for bringing people along is not left to one person with one set of standards or viewpoints but rather is shared by a team of managers bringing to the table diverse standards and viewpoints.

I sincerely hope that qualified gay management will be available to be a mentor because his or her presence both in the process and on the management team certainly sends the correct message that people are judged by their work and not by their orientation. If no such person is visible at your organization, then alternatives to consider include looking outside your organization for a qualified civic leader, consultant, or professor to participate (and hopefully help encourage someone to step up to the plate from the home team).

Another strategy that I advocate for sending the right message in your ranks is one called "coming-out coaches." This term may be new to some, but the concept has been around in an underground fashion for many years. Coming-out coaches are people who have themselves come out at work, worked through whatever difficulties that may have caused, and now feel comfortable enough and ready to help others who are struggling with the same decisions. These people are not advocates of coming out in terms of trying to talk people into it, nor are they qualified psychological counselors. They are just regular employees who lend support simply by their willingness to attest to the fact that "I did it and you can do it, too."

HR managers can help promote such an informal network of coaches in their own workplace and help it to grow by making it available to neighboring enterprises. Of course, an employee alliance is the number-one source for providing people willing to serve in this role for others. Both mentoring and coming-out coach strategies are hugely cooperative efforts between the employee network and the organization.

External Outreach

The organization is not going to know about the Human Rights Campaign's *Corporate Equality Index,* the National Gay and Lesbian Task Force, the Center for Gender Sanity, Out & Equal, the conventions sponsored by Gay Business World, *Echelon* Magazine, or the dozens of other sources for outreach, information, and exposure that exist in the world. Appendix I lists many resources for the employee network and for the organization, several of which can help the employee network fulfill its mission statement and objectives as well as give organizations outstanding ways to fully leverage and take advantage of this aspect of their inclusive policies.

Your organizations can't participate in matters important to the employee network if they don't know what they are, how to get involved, or, especially, what's in it for them if they do.

Supplier Diversity

The reality of supplier diversity programs beginning to actively encompass sexual orientation and gender identity is very new and definitely one of the impetuses for wanting to update this book.

A recent issue of the new *Echelon* magazine includes a story about how all of the bleeding-edge change at IBM around sexual orientation and gender identity (IBM has been first in so many ways around this aspect of diversity, one loses count of all their initiatives) has resulted in Big Blue unveiling the first procurement and diversity development program directed at LGBT-owned companies.[1] The program is intended to enable IBM to purchase more products and use more services provided by gay- and lesbian-run businesses.

A project right now, in today's world, to investigate the way that IBM arrived at this supplier-diversity initiative, to see how it's going, to identify suppliers, and then to encourage your own organization to initiate a similar program is a very doable thing for the employee network. It would not only be good for the organization as a way to demonstrate inclusion and therefore build market share in the LGBT community (see Chapter 7) but would also certainly be a boon to small businesses run by LGBT people. It's another way that the employee group would benefit a number of different constituencies, including itself.

Help HR

The employee group can take a proactive role in helping human resources professionals do their jobs even better. If HR representatives, for example, don't know what to do to help their gay employees feel safer and able to be more productive, maybe it's because no gay person knows how to reach out and tell them and they don't know how to ask. The employee group can proactively reach out to every single HR rep in the organization to find out where they stand relative to sexual orientation and gender identity in the workplace. Do they need information? Are they comfortable dealing with this aspect of diversity? Are they someone closeted gay people can reach out to and discuss workplace issues with? The employee group can be—and should be—a conduit for communication and information.

Be a PFLAG

One of the organizations listed in the resources appendix (Appendix I), and one that I am particularly fond of, is PFLAG, which stands for Parents, Families and Friends of Lesbians and Gays. This is an organization comprised mostly of heterosexual people who found out that a close friend or beloved family member was gay or transgender and they had to deal with it. Or maybe they didn't have to deal with it, but they chose to as opposed to writing that person, a son, a daughter, a mom, a cousin, a best friend, out of their lives.

In the workplace, it's not only gay people who can feel alienated due to their sexual orientation. I meet and talk with people all the time who are straight and who are in terrible pain and conflict because of their attitudes and beliefs about sexual orientation and then find out someone they really care about is gay. The employee network can be a sort of an internal PFLAG to such people by working hard to communicate an awareness that these feelings sometimes exist in people and they have resources (including PFLAG itself) that they can help employees in this situation find.

A Built-In Market Research Firm

Employee groups have always constituted a tremendous resource in terms of the organization understanding what potential exists for their products and/or services to the "gay community." Certainly one of the most positive aspects of awareness and openness about orientation from a strictly dollars-and-sense standpoint is that a whole untapped market is ready, willing, and able to patronize organizations willing to meet them halfway. Telling the organization where this halfway point is and how the organization can get there is a powerful strength of an employee network group.

In short, don't tell me that since you got the nondiscrimination policy changed and won domestic partner benefits there's left nothing to do.

We Are All in This Together

It is important that employee groups formed around sexual orientation remember a few things. First, heterosexuality is an orientation too. Second, not everyone is in the same place where coming out of the closet is concerned, and requirements for anonymity and privacy must be respected (while we work toward helping people feel they don't have to live in the closet).

Third, "subcommunities" within the so-called "LGBT community" are starting to emerge. I'm talking about people of color, black people and others, who are also gay and bring a whole other dimension of awareness and inclusion because it is different to be black and gay, or Latino and gay, than it is to be white and gay.

Fourth, in this day and age where people are adamantly demanding that their religious selves also be acknowledged by their workplaces, there doesn't have to be an automatic disconnect between groups formed around sexual orientation and gender identity and those formed around religion and spirituality.

Say It Loud

I'm a child of the 1960s, having been born in 1957, and so I remember clearly what was called at the time a "black militant cry" of "say it loud, I'm Black and I'm proud!" Because of this, I was charmed by a report released by the National Gay and Lesbian Task Force in conjunction with the National Black Lesbian and Gay Leadership Forum, former NGLTF Policy Institute director Urvashi Vaid, and researchers and leaders from the black LGBT community called "Say It Loud: I'm Black and I'm Proud; Black Pride Survey 2000"[2] I was charmed because of the clever way the word *proud* referred to both black pride and gay pride.

This report is fascinating because it discusses in great detail (and by "great" I mean both "a lot" and "it's really good") the differentiations in family structure, political behavior, experiences of racism and homophobia, and the policy priorities of black gay people. Of particular importance is the evidence of a kind of broadly accepted cultural denial in the black community that there are any gay black people, which is almost a throw-back to general reactions to gay people in the United States less than twenty years ago. What I mean is that there are certainly issues to being black or gay in America, but being gay in the black community is an additional struggle. Within the Hispanic community, machismo also seems to put pressures on Latino gay, lesbian, and transgender people that transcend what they have to deal with from the rest of society. Therefore, great opportunities exist for cultural awareness being cross-pollinated with sexual orientation and gender-identity awareness that most employee organizations have not even scratched the surface of.

By the year 2050, white people will be a minority in the United States.[3] Anyone interested in sexual orientation as an aspect of workplace diversity certainly should read this report for the following reason: There is a huge misconception about gay people that we are all, every single one of us, white. We're not. We come in all shapes, sizes, colors, ethnicities, races, religions, you name it, and it would be worthwhile for employee networks to start proactively bringing people who are other than white, male or female, to the table. We have a lot to learn about one another even within the strict confines of "the gay community."*

RELIGION

A person can't do what I do for a living and expect to get through the day without having to discuss the ways in which religion and sexual orientation intersect. Frankly, it isn't usually anything resembling goodwill and cooperation. People seem determined to use scripture

---

*The term *gay community* is one that I use, but often with mixed feelings. I don't really believe that there is a gay community any more than I think there is a straight community. I understand the term's place in being able to conveniently group people together when you want to refer to them as a whole, but the more we appreciate the diversity inherent in all people with a sexual orientation (which, of course, is all people) the harder it is to think this term has any meaning at all. However, many people are using it . . . so I guess it still does.

(or their interpretation thereof) to prove beyond a doubt that gay people are "lesser than," immoral, irreligious, and undeserving of civil rights or simple human dignity. I don't know where these people expect us to go. Maybe they expect us to crawl back into the closet. I often wonder, though, if we were to accommodate them on this point, what would they have to complain about then? I think that some people need, and want, to have gays to demonize. It seems to give them a reason to get up in the morning, and for that, I pity them.

However, as I explained earlier, among people 10 percent are so far to the left and 10 percent are so far to the right that they can't ever hear me or want to. It's the 80 percent in the middle that I'm aiming at and always have. And I've learned that within that 80 percent are people who consider the religion in their lives to be one of the top three most important things about them and their existence, so you'd think that I'd find them equally intransigent, but I'm happy to say that I don't always find them to be so and I've hit upon a theory of cooperation between employee groups founded on religion and those founded upon sexual orientation and gender identity.

Random House/Webster's defines "religion" as "a set of beliefs concerning the cause, nature, and purpose of the universe, usually involving devotions and rituals and often containing a moral code for human conduct." It defines "spirituality" as "the quality or fact of being spiritual; of or pertaining to the soul or spirit as distinguished from the physical nature. The spirit is the seat of moral behavior."

To me, the most important distinction between religion and spirituality is that religion imposes a moral code and spirituality encourages moral behavior. Religion is a rule written by others; spirituality is an intention determined by oneself. Spirituality doesn't interfere with or undermine personal religious beliefs; it focuses on common elements existing in all religious traditions, addresses transcendent issues in an empowering fashion, and doesn't hold with dogma, values, qualities, or specific creeds.

Why do I mention all this? Because in short (as it's really a wholly separate subject and subtext of diversity in the workplace) an organization will have fewer conflicts between people if they allow employees to feed their desire for meaning at work by forming employee groups around spirituality instead of religion. Frankly, religion in the workplace is a sort of code for "Christianity" in the workplace, and limiting an employee group in this way is ill-advised. There are, at last count, more than 9,000 known "religions" on the planet. If you have a Christian Employee Network, your chances of alienating other people are really quite high.

However, if an organization does encourage employees from all faiths who wish to form a "religious" employee network (or several) to do so from the standpoint of spirituality and not religion, then you have not only a chance for more success on that basis but also an enormous opportunity to engender positive communication between an employee group founded upon the human characteristics of sexual orientation and gender identity and one formed around spirituality.

Approached in this way, as I have been helping several client companies to do, employee groups can work together on projects and events that represent both of their interests. For example, it's not unusual that a group formed around spirituality would want to hold a sort of "health fair" for underserved members of the community to get access to information about health care or even blood tests or mammograms by raising funds for this purpose. Well, people in the gay community have a long-standing interest in seeing to it that gay and transgender people get information and access to care about HIV and other sexually transmitted and bloodborne diseases and breast cancer. So working to make blood tests and mammograms available would be in the network's common interest and something they could do together.

What I'm saying here is that we needn't always start with the point of view that people who are "religious" and people who are gay have nothing to say to one another, never care about the same things, never work toward the same goals, never find common ground.

They do. They can. They should.

Chapter 7

LGBTs and the Marketplace: Progressiveness Pays

What defines progressiveness in the marketplace? I think progressiveness is reflected by a slight but palpable shift from a reactive (let's avoid the negatives) to a proactive (what can we do before the competition does?) mind-set. By finding ways to get ahead of an oncoming curve, in this case the growing awareness and visibility around sexual orientation, companies can enhance their profitability. The potential benefits include gaining market share, improving their competitive advantage for labor and patronage, and taking full advantage of their greatest resource—all the people, gay and straight, who work for them.

Diversity management is viewed now more than ever as a business issue and less as strictly a human resources issue. The distinction is a crucial one. Some shadowy relationship between taking care of your people and their resulting performance has always been acknowledged, but it was never considered an empirical cause and effect. However, thanks to people such as Dr. Edward Hubbard, these changes are no longer just anecdotal; they can be proven with data.

In his book *Measuring Diversity Results,* Hubbard presents a workable model for giving a quantitative value to diversity efforts in the workplace.[1] His tools include more than 100 formulas to report the effect that diversity initiatives have on bottom-line performance. He also provides ways of assessing the return on investment of such efforts, ways to track and monitor changes due to diversity initiatives, and ways to ensure that the initiatives are connected in meaningful ways to the business case for the programs.

When your organization does positively acknowledge sexual orientation, can you expect to be penalized, in real time, in the marketplace? The answer is a resounding no. Furthermore, it appears that discriminatory practices fail an organization money-wise and progressiveness in this area actually, literally, pays.

To this point, in the previous two editions of this book I used my own state's (Colorado) passing of Proposition Two (which invalidated all local ordinances that included sexual orientation as a protected status in employment, housing, and public accommodations) as an example of a place that suffered a documented loss of convention and tourism revenues in excess of $120 million. The fact that Proposition Two was later overturned by the Supreme Court never helped to recover a nickel of those funds. The fact that it was the Supreme Court who had to overturn Proposition Two did nothing to improve Colorado's image as an intolerant place. Actually, Colorado is no more—or less—intolerant on issues related to sexual orientation than any other place I've been in the United States or Canada. Although I will admit that Colorado Springs does have more than its share of hard-line, religious right, ultraconservative organizations which contribute to that discriminatory image.

Portland, Oregon, lost $15 million in convention revenue after an antigay initiative was put on a ballot, even though the initiative itself was defeated, and Cobb County, Georgia, gave up an estimated $10 million in Olympic Games revenue when fair-minded people convinced the Olympic Committee to move the volleyball competition to another county because of Cobb's exclusionary practices.

However, one doesn't have to look far to find evidence that discrimination, or a reputation for it, is bad business. For example, a *Denver Post* story from March 22, 2004, titled "'Intolerant' tag deters businesses from Utah"[2] told of a biotechnology company CEO who wanted to relocate from Tucson to Salt Lake City but couldn't because he couldn't convince his people to leave Arizona for Utah. Whether deserved or not, Utah has the reputation for being unwelcoming to people who are not Mormon or conservative in their views and values. So business won't come. This is occasionally very bad for business, and it is certainly bad for Utah, which sacrifices both jobs and tax revenues to its reputation for being a closed-minded place to live and work.

When the Walt Disney Corporation implemented domestic partner benefits they were the subject of a large, organized boycott attempt by a particular religious organization. The boycott failed and the company posted better-than-expected profits and revenues as compared to the previous year's same fiscal period. Americans do not boycott in the name of discrimination; they boycott in the name of stopping it.

People make significant investments in themselves, and when they go out into the working world, they expect return on those investments. They also want to do business with companies that share their values, and it's becoming more evident that inclusion is a value shared by all sorts of people on all kinds of levels. Any decisions by an employer of any type that are reflected overtly in published hiring policies or covertly in the initiatives of the company to provide for only a certain race, gender, or orientation will result in an enormous loss of competitive positioning for the company. As more organizations offer protection and equitable benefits, people working in less-progressive companies get up and move to them.

Look at it this way. If any corporation tried to turn back the clock to 1940 or so and told all its black employees that they were unwelcome to use the same toilets or eat in the same cafeteria as whites, that organization could reasonably expect trouble in the form of lowered morale, lessened productivity, and loss of profitability. Most if not all of its black employees would walk out the door. Similarly, if any corporation or university publicly stated that no woman working within it should expect to rise in the ranks higher than administrative assistant or assistant professor, the organization could not feign surprise if the women working there gave less than their all or left altogether. Either scenario would probably lead to public outrage and boycotting of the company's products. But this is exactly the kind of treatment faced by workers on the basis of their sexual orientation. It is not only nonprogressive but incredibly wasteful, and it can cost dearly. On the other hand, taking advantage of our society's penchant for fairness and nondiscrimination can be very profitable indeed.

THE BUSINESS CASE: AN EXAMPLE

The business case for inclusion of all known kinds of human diversity, including sexual orientation and gender identity, can also still be expressed in words as well as in numbers. At Deluxe Corporation, the largest financial printer in the world, they laid down the following challenges for the organization:

- If we meet the needs of an increasingly diverse customer marketplace because we are constantly researching untapped markets in the United States and they are primarily composed of people of color, people with disabilities, people over forty-five years old, people whose orientation is in the minority, among others, and
- If we understand the new skilled workers, because in the United States, by the year 2005, the net new entrants into the workforce will be 85 percent minorities, women, and immigrants, and
- If we incorporate diversity into our globalization efforts because we are looking at regions well beyond our North American borders, and
- If we better use our workforce, because underutilization of the workforce is related to a loss in productivity and ultimately to our bottom-line earnings, then we will succeed in
  1. Fully using the talents and experiences of our associates to maximize our productivity in meeting the challenges of the increasingly diverse marketplace
  2. Providing continuous quality improvement through understanding our new skilled workers and effectively exchanging knowledge with our current and new business partners
  3. Being a global leader in providing the best services and products to our customers
  4. Being the employer of choice for our associates
  5. Being the model of the best business practices in our industries
  6. Gaining an abundance of competitive advantages[3]

Shell Exploration and Production Company (SEPCo), an affiliate of Shell Oil Company, has developed a Diversity Performance Standard whose purpose is to be a roadmap for creating an environment of inclusion within the company.[4]

This document has two focal points. The first is a matrix that SEPCo has created to diagram "a performance standard and assessment tool to help achieve an environment of inclusion in which Diversity excellence promotes business success."[5] The matrix is comprised of the steps that business units can and should take to measure their performance in, and relative to, diversity management in the SEPCo workplaces.

These steps fall into the categories of leadership and commitment; employee engagement; work relationships; opportunities and fairness; demographics; family and personal life balance; and community. The stages that each business unit is encouraged to pass through for each category are (in order) awareness of, understanding of, acceptance of, and commitment to diversity in each.

What's remarkable about the document, beyond its being a state-of-the-art examination of the practical business aspects of workplace diversity, is the obvious amount of time, energy, and resources that went into it. Anyone fortunate enough to analyze the document comes away with a much deeper understanding of how diversity impacts the bottom-line of an organization for everyone, regardless of job title or function or place in the hierarchy.

Why does an organization such as Shell Exploration and Production put so many people, so much time, and so much money into this task?

> One reason that valuing Diversity is so important to our business is that the *only way* to truly succeed is to fully utilize the talents of every person in our company. That is how we can achieve both our collective and individual potential. To do otherwise is not acceptable at a time when we need all hands on deck. Without the sense of belonging, respect and value that all individuals require, we risk losing our most valuable assets . . . the talents of our people and our reputation in the community.[6]

WHAT'S AT STAKE IN DOLLARS AND CENTS

The gay market segment is, according to Mulryan/Nash and the Simmons Market Research Bureau, one of the fastest, if not the fastest-growing demographic for products and services in the United States.[7] That statement was true when first written in 1998, and it's still true today. Since 1997, which was the first year that ad revenues in LGBT media topped $100 million dollars, they have continued to grow in that market at a rate of more than 25 percent per year.

As previously noted in this book, Witeck-Combs and Harris Interactive reported that there are 15 million self-identified gays and lesbian people as of the 2000 U.S. Census and surveys done in 2002.[8] According to their report, focused strictly on the market implications of these population numbers, buying power for the LGBT community was $451 billion in 2002 and is projected to reach $608 billion by 2007, a cumulative increase of more than 34 percent from 2002 figures. By comparison, African-American spending power is projected to reach $852.8 billion by 2007; Latino spending power projected to reach $927.1 billion; and Asian-American spending power to be at $454.9 billion.[9]

Conversations about the spending power of any portion of the population can often be a double-edged sword, and this is as true for the LGBT market as for any I've ever studied. On one hand, $451 billion to $608 billion in potential revenue are impressive sums that cannot, and probably should not, be ignored by marketers and advertisers. On the other hand, a myth survives about the affluence of gay people that is often used against them to try to demonstrate that they are some sort of "elite" group using their economic and political muscle to get whatever they want. I haven't noticed a whole lot of political clout, given the inability of gay people, even under a president like Clinton, to get the Employment Non-Discrimination Act passed or do away with don't ask, don't tell, but people who say these things are seldom likely to let the truth get in the way.

The truth is that, according to University of Massachusetts economist Professor Lee Badget, gay men earn from 11 to 27 percent less than their straight counterparts.[10] Other research and national, statistically valid polls have indicated that the gay and lesbian population in the United States is similar to the population as a whole in terms of income and other demographics.

The reason for targeting marketing efforts toward LGBT people is not because they are better than another demographic you may target but because they represent the same sort of revenue potential as any other market.

What's Important to LGBT Consumers

If you want to leverage the LGBT market, you have to first know what's important to it. The research shows that the LGBT market is among the most attention-starved, loyal, and easy mark for marketers to build early dominance in if they take the plunge.[11] There is great truth in the theory that the gay market is open to organizations that take its requirements into consideration, both as employees and as patrons.

What follows is a description of what matters to the LGBT market, and I think that this information is significant not only in and of itself, but also because it can now be gathered with a great deal more reliability than just targeting people who subscribe to magazines.[12]

- LGBT consumers have a deeper trust for products and brands that target gay consumers, but even more for products offered by companies that have progressive policies toward all employees, including but not limited to LGBT employees.
- Fifty-six percent of all LGBT people sampled agreed that they more often trust brands from progressive companies, with 41 percent reporting that they strongly agree.
- The most important public policy issues to LGBT consumers are
  —Protections for LGBT people from workplace discrimination
  —Passing laws that discourage antigay bias crimes
  —The right of gays to parent, including adoption
  —The right to civil marriage for same-sex couples
  —Securing federal benefits such as social security, pensions, and family and medical leave
  —HIV/AIDS funding, care, treatment, and prevention
  —Specifically including gender identity in all public and private protection policies
  —Ending the military's "Don't Ask, Don't Tell" policy
  —Research for women's health issues, including breast and cervical cancer
  —Equal treatment of binational couples
  —Securing benefits administered at the state level
- By a ratio of 47 percent (LGBT) to 18 percent (heterosexual), gay consumers are more likely to make a purchasing decision based on their awareness of a company's diversity policies.
- With all other factors being equal (such as price, quality, value, and function) LGBT consumers were more likely to favor one organization's products and services over another if they knew that the salesperson or representative was also LGBT. This was 56 percent of the total for financial services; 51 percent for

health care; 49 percent for large purchases such as cars and houses; 42 percent for everyday purchases such as groceries; and 42 percent for computers or home entertainment products.
- Eighty percent of LGBT respondents to an August 2001 poll said they would be willing to recommend a particular company or vendor to others based on favorable inclusion policies. This was compared to 26 percent of heterosexual respondents to the same question.
- Fifty-six percent of LGBT respondents in the August 2001 poll said they "shop at stores that advertise to people like me" as opposed to 43 percent of heterosexual respondents.
- Ninety-four percent of LGBT people said they shop at stores that make them feel welcome as compared to 88 percent of heterosexual people.

What should leap out from these various statistics is that the growing atmosphere of awareness and visibility encourages people who were once considered to be very much on the fringes to be willing and able to make spending decisions based on information about a particular organization's policies toward people—in most cases, toward all people. It behooves organizations to not only have such progressive policies but also to publicize them, because as I noted before, the amount of negative backlash you may experience from small numbers of exclusionary thinkers is far outweighed by the positive results you can expect in a more aware world.

Bob Witeck of Witeck-Combs put it this way:

> In the past few years, we have learned that buying behavior has common threads for gay and non-gay consumers alike. Gay men and lesbians consider the same factors as others do, but they now expect high standards of respect and equal inclusion in the market and workplace. Companies that understand these attitudes will successfully communicate their values and market their products to increasingly visible gay households.[13]

How do companies that understand these attitudes manifest this communication? The answer is through advertising.

ADVERTISING TO THE LGBT MARKET

When I was coming of age there was absolutely no such thing as a gay newspaper or magazine that was targeted at me, a young, gay, professional woman with a graduate degree and a decent income. The only papers I remember being able to get my hands on if I visited Greenwich Village in New York City or one of the few gay bars on Long Island were all about the bar scene and weren't much more than mimeographed pages (remember mimeographing? If you do, then now you know about how old I am) stapled together and passed around between friends because there were never many to go around.

When I started Common Ground in 1993, only about twenty gay-oriented newspapers in major cities and two national magazines had enough sustainable revenues and subscribers to keep publishing. Today, there are more than 100 newspapers in cities and towns large and small and seven or more national, gay-focused magazines, with new ones popping up all the time. Of course, even the mainstream media outlets are sensitive to the fact that not everyone out there reading, watching, or listening to them is heterosexual.

An online consumer survey done by Witeck-Combs and Harris Interactive in July 2003 reported that gay consumers tend to read and view many of the same media as their heterosexual counterparts, but across the board they favor lifestyle/fashion, home decorating and design magazines, news magazines, and premium cable networks more than their nongay counterparts.[14]

Sixty percent of gay individuals consistently read magazines such as *Newsweek* and *Time,* while the same is true for about 45 percent of heterosexuals.

Gay magazines such as *The Advocate, Out,* and *Curve* are read regularly by one-third of gay people in the United States, and close to half of those surveyed said that they also favor online gay channels such as PlanetOut.com or Gay.com that allow for a certain amount of anonymity in viewing. One in five gay people report regularly reading their local gay newspaper in the city or town where they live or work.

What all of this means, of course, is that literally dozens of channels exist for marketers and advertisers to ply their wares in an attempt to attract LGBT people to their products and services. The buying power of the LGBT market, when combined with their awareness of who's doing what in terms of corporate and public policy and with their media savvy, make this a market rich with revenue possibilities for those organizations quick enough, bold enough, and smart enough to go after them.

A recent article by Valerie Seckler titled "Targeting Gays: Affluent Market Largely Ignored"[15] discusses the starts and stops that organizations are experiencing in going after the LGBT market and what opportunities might have been missed because of them. In it she reports:

- Out of 15 million gay men and lesbians with a perceived buying power as of 2003 of about $500 billion, lesbians make up 6.3 million, with spending clout of about $200 billion.
- Because of stereotyping, lesbians are left out of the advertising mix by the fashion industry even though, as noted earlier, they are among the population that favors lifestyle/fashion media. The stereotyping is that all lesbians ever wear are sweatpants, jeans, and flannel shirts. This applies one standard of interests and appearance to a group of more than 6 million people, which is, of course, silly.
- Fashion brands such as Kenneth Cole, Dolce and Gabbana, Calvin Klein, and others are bypassing the traditional media and putting images they believe will appeal to LGBT consumers in their catalogs and then are using direct-market research to find their target audience. In their huge holiday catalog at the end of 2003, Abercrombie and Fitch portrayed two women in a commitment ceremony wearing their duds.

Seckler's article goes on to discuss the fact that gay people don't, by and large, want to see heterocentric ads in their "gay media," but they likewise do not value subtle or ambiguous ads in the mainstream media that they have "a feeling" are targeted to them but can't be quite sure. Gay consumers have, in the past few years, experienced freedoms and increased recognition beyond the imaginations of those who grew up when I did. They are out of the closet at work; they are out to their family and friends; they are out politically, economically, and socially. They are starting to demand to be out in the media, and successful marketing campaigns will jump all over that. These campaigns will be rewarded by the brand loyalty mentioned earlier in this chapter and, if done right, they will not have to fear alienating the mainstream market in the process. Marketers should keep in mind the growing familiarity of straight people with gay people in their lives and all the statistics that point to a definite awareness and belief in the mainstream marketplace that inclusion is good.

BEST PRACTICES IN ADVERTISING

More data on LGBT response to advertising come from Greenfield OnLine, Simmons Research, Witeck-Combs, the Commercial Closet, and Harris (Harris Polls On Line).*[16] What they tell us, among other things, is that the factors that most influence LGBT consumers in making decisions about brand loyalty are the following:

1. Whether a company advertises in gay media
2. Whether a company demonstrates effective corporate citizenship (i.e., gives back)
3. Whether a company establishes and publicizes progressive policies toward LGBT employees
4. Whether a company shows gay images in advertising
5. Whether a company shows gay images in packaging

Between 1999 and 2001, 84 percent of LGBT people asked said that they always order drinks by brand names they are loyal to (as compared to 41 percent of the nongay respondents). Seventy-seven percent had in that two-year period switched brands to companies with a positive stance toward LGBT people; and 74 percent were less likely to buy a product versus 42 percent of heterosexuals if a company advertised on shows with negative messages about LGBT people.[17]

What does this mean? It means that people—all kinds of people—tend to vote with their wallets.

The first companies to jump on the gay advertisement bandwagons were in the liquor and cigarette industries, which should come as no surprise based on what I stated previously about all of the publications that I could get my hands on having all to do with the bar scene. Now, of course, many other outlets in print, online, and telecommuni-

---

*A complete list and description of organizations you can look to for help with marketing/advertising strategies to the LGBT market is in Appendix I.

cations media are available, and so many different types of organizations have what are called gay marketing strategies. The list is long, and it's getting longer every day. Just as of Q1, 2004, it includes Apple, IBM, AT&T, American Airlines, Disney Corporation, Calvin Klein, Levi's, Naya, Crate & Barrel, Barnes & Noble, HBO, MTV, Showtime, America Online, American Express, Visa, Wells Fargo, Wachovia, John Hancock, E*Trade Financial, United Airlines, Avis, Philips, Verizon, SBC Communications, Subaru, Volvo, Jaguar, Mercedes-Benz, Land Rover, Saturn, Ford, Absolut, GlaxoSmithKline, Roxane Laboratories, Serono, and Merck. I'm sure there are more as I'm writing this; I'm positive there will be more by the time this book comes out.

The names on this list are interesting on a variety of levels. First, I can't help noticing all the financial services companies that are on the current list. For the longest time, people swore that companies such as AMEX or John Hancock would never advertise to the gay community and they'd never have inclusive nondiscrimination policies or domestic partner benefits either. In fact, just about every publicly held financial services company on old-world, ultraconservative Wall Street has both the policies and the benefits.

As for images in advertising, I am a perfect example of why this works. About six years ago a friend recommended her AMEX/IDS agent-broker to my partner and me when we were shopping for a life insurance annuity plan. The friend is gay, but we didn't know the sexual orientation of the person she recommended. When that agent came to our house, sat down, and whipped out all the fancy literature, she didn't even have time to start explaining the plan when I said, "We'll take it." Why did I say this? Because the brochure she took out showed two women on the cover sitting at their kitchen table considering the family budget. It was all I needed to see to know that this company understood us as consumers and what we needed to protect ourselves and our assets.

In May 2003, Commercial Closet posted an article called "Volvo Bids for Gay Families" written by Michael Wilke.[18] In it he writes,

> Gay families, previously hidden away in the suburbs, are now starting to make their way into advertising. Volvo Cars of North America takes its heritage of safety and family appeal a step further by introducing its new SUV with the first national car ad picturing a happy gay couple posed with a child or dog.

[The] print campaign [shows] . . . two men and a baby, another with a woman embracing her pregnant partner—each with the headline, "Whether you're starting a family or creating one as you go." . . . The text of each ad reads, "Some families are carefully planned. Others, you just meet along the way. Whoever makes up your family, think about making Volvo a part of it."

Why did Volvo run these ads? Because, according to their executive vice president, Thomas Andersson, "We're targeting people with modern family values. It's a value set, and the Volvo-minded consumer is very diverse. 'Family' is much more than the traditional family."[19]

Volvo is certainly not alone in recognizing the realities of their market and being among the first to try to leverage it. The people who are walking in Volvo's footsteps and the places they are doing it might surprise you for now; in a few years, it will all seem commonplace.

For example, my research for this chapter turned up a story that ran in the *South Florida Sun-Sentinel* of Fort Lauderdale, titled "Builders Tailor Homes, Marketing to Interest Gay Buyers."[20] The story starts, "Hope to lure high-income buyers, some South Florida developers are building luxury projects that will appeal to the gay market." It goes on to discuss the research these developers are doing to figure out what "will appeal to the gay market" and then how they are building and advertising their projects to gay people. Furthermore, they are not just advertising in the "gay media"; their ads are very much in mainstream media in the South Florida market.

The residual effect of projects such as these is that they are occurring in areas known for being welcoming to all types of people, and where gay people in particular are concerned, entire communities of people of all sexual orientations and gender identities are being created and supported which will, over time, prove that people don't have to live in cultural ghettos of their, or someone else's, making. Once people understand, through exposure, awareness, or training, internal (within an organization) or external (public relations/marketing) diversity efforts, that what we all have in common is our differences, consultants like me will be unnecessary. This will take a while, of course—but it's a goal worth working toward.

So, how should you go about this if you want to pursue the LGBT market? The Commercial Closet Association put out a set of best practice guidelines for advertising to LGBT people.[21] A summary of the guidelines follows:

1. Be inclusive and diverse—make images of LGBT people as clear as possible; don't be subtle. Make sure that different types of families are reflected, as well as people of different ages, races, and so on. Use language familiar to the gay community, such as referring to people "coming out."
2. Avoid positioning gay or transgender people as a perceived threat in order to get a laugh. What this means is that you should not play with stereotypes about LGBT people—how they supposedly look or behave—in order to sell your products.
3. Do good research. There is nothing illegal about including questions about a person's sexual orientation or gender identity and then trying to ascertain what their buying habits may be because of it. Right now, Witeck-Combs and Harris, Simmons, and others known for working in this market (although not exclusively in any of their cases) are doing this sort of work. Certainly, you can, and should, leverage their knowledge. Also, you can incorporate these sorts of interrogatories into the market research that you do.
4. Go national. The most recent Census (2000) showed that gay people live in 99.4 percent of all counties in the United States. This isn't just about New York, San Francisco, and Key West. People in all parts of the country are aware that not everyone is straight and they are aware enough to appreciate niche advertising even if they are not the niche in the ad.
5. Be confident about what you are doing. If you get some negative feedback, and perhaps in the short term you should expect that, don't back down. The market research proves that ultimately your campaign, if well conceived, will reap positive benefits.
6. Make sure senior management is visible in its endorsement of the advertisements.
7. Use focus groups made up of many LGBT people to get feedback on whether your message is hitting home as you intended. This is a perfect way to utilize the existence of an employee network formed around sexual orientation and/or gender identity.
8. Don't hesitate to provide internal diversity training specifically focused on sexual orientation and gender identity for those peo-

ple designing your campaign, implementing it, and who are seen as accountable for it.

A NEW KIND OF SUPPLIER DIVERSITY

In spring 2004, IBM introduced America's first LGBT vendor program. IBM has long been in front of the curve to be inclusive of LGBT people in its internal policies. In fact, it included the words sexual orientation in its nondiscrimination policy in 1976, and it's not a stretch to say that it took almost a decade for any of its corporate peers to catch up. IBM has also led the charge in advertising and marketing to the gay community in all sorts of media. So perhaps it is not a surprise that they are the first to incorporate LGBT into supplier diversity, but whatever they are doing in this realm, others can learn from.

For me it's just interesting, and a bit groundbreaking, to be able to point to a real example of inclusive supplier diversity that specifically counts LGBT businesses in the supplier bucket. For years, of course, I've been touting supplier diversity as an aspect of the business case for inclusion on the basis of sexual orientation, but until March 2004, I certainly had no specific example of LGBT inclusion that I could share with my clients. I feel certain that by the time I see this book in print, other corporations will have followed IBM down this road, so although I regret not being able to feature more than one program in these pages, I have a feeling that it's all going to work out to the good before long.

IBM is partnering with the National Gay & Lesbian Chamber of Commerce (NGLCC) to launch its procurement and diversity development program directed at LGBT-owned companies. Simply put, through this program IBM hopes to purchase and use more products and services provided by LGBT-run businesses.[22]

The method that IBM will use to initiate networking between LGBT vendors will be an online trade fair, the first of which will roll out in November 2004. To date, ninety LGBT businesses have used this virtual trade floor to set up their virtual booths, where they describe themselves, their products, and their services. So, if you are hearing about this for the first time and you are an LGBT-run business or a representative of a company looking to follow this extraordinary lead, visit the IBM Web site for more information. I have a feeling, a good one, that this information will be valuable and valid for years to come.

"THE EQUALITY PRINCIPLES"
AND SHAREHOLDER ACTIVISM

In the mid-1990s, an organization formed called the Equality Project, which focused itself on identifying companies that adhered to a ten-point list called "The Equality Principles."[23] The complete text of these principles is available on the Internet at <www.hrc.org>. They speak to the specific inclusion of language pertaining to sexual orientation and gender identity in an organization's nondiscrimination policy, as well as to a person's real or perceived health status or disability. They also speak to offering domestic partner benefits and to offering education programs that pointedly cover orientation and identity. Externally focused programs and policies, such as advertising efforts and charitable contributions, are also covered in the principles.

The Equality Principles set a high bar of standards for inclusion, as does the Human Rights Campaign's Corporate Equality Index,[24] which rates companies on their inclusion policies similar to, but not as comprehensive as, those set forth in the Principles. Still, getting a good rating in either scale can help an organization that wishes to proactively demonstrate inclusion on this basis and is another way to work with your employee network to get your organization involved with both the Equality Project and HRC.*

Until about the beginning of 2002 or so, I'd say that both the Corporate Equality Index and the Equality Project made do with just collecting data and rating the performances of, mostly, the Fortune 1000 relative to the Principles or the Index. But in the past year or two, thanks to a phenomenon called shareholder activism that has been steadily gaining momentum and allies as a way to engender social change through change at some of our biggest corporations, the people involved are not content to sit back any longer. They're starting to drive changes proactively.

---

*See Appendix I for contact information.

Take for example the case of Cracker Barrel stores, owned by CBRL Group, Inc. In the 1990s it was not at all unusual for people to be fired by the corporation or a given store and the reason, clearly stated on a firing notice, was "employee is gay." The company once circulated a memo saying that all Cracker Barrel employees must exhibit "normal, heterosexual values" in order to remain employed.[25] Headquartered in Tennessee, with a preponderance of stores in other southern states that don't have any laws or ordinances for employment protection on the basis of sexual orientation, it was actually Cracker Barrel's legal right to fire gay people and send around memos like this. Repulsive perhaps, but legal.

In 2003, however, Cracker Barrel changed its tune as well as its nondiscrimination policy to include sexual orientation in response to protests, boycotts, and, especially, a campaign by shareholders who worked for a decade to pass a shareholder resolution demanding the change.

Cracker Barrel is not the first, or only, organization that has been encouraged to be more inclusive of sexual orientation (although not, as yet, gender identity), but one of the most significant things about what happened in this case of shareholder activism is that the New York City Employees' Retirement System, which controlled (at the time of the resolution) 189,000 shares of CBRL, was an ally in the resolution fight. Since that time, the New York pension plan has brought similar influence to bear on Wal-Mart, JC Penney, and FedEx, to name but three.

There is every reason to think that this kind of shareholder activism will gain more momentum in line with gains made in employee policies, employee education which spurs both awareness and acceptance, and the market clout of the LGBT population and its allies all over the world. As Cyndi Lauper put it succinctly, "money changes everything."

CLIENT-ACQUISITION EDUCATION

Commercial Closet's best practices guidelines for advertising to the LGBT market and "The Equality Principles" allude to internal education in support of external outreach or revenue-generating efforts. Certainly, education on the subject of sexual orientation and gender identity for employees of all kinds is valuable in and of itself because there is such a dearth of it available now, but education with an eye toward enhancing revenue or image may be slightly different than what is offered as part of a diversity initiative. This is called client-acquisition education, and although it hasn't been embraced (yet) by many organizations, it is an idea that may have been ahead of itself when I first wrote about it in 1998 and now the world may be catching up to it.

Client-acquisition education consists of deconstructing sexual orientation to the level and for the purposes of understanding how a person's sexual orientation (especially if not in the majority) affects that person's decisions relative to products and services.

For example, if an oil/petroleum company wanted to appeal to this market, could they produce something called "Gay Gas"? If a company that makes products for babies wanted to capitalize on what is being referred to as the "Gayby Boom," could there be a market for gay diapers or gay formula? On one hand, such suggestions are preposterous, but on the other, they are not. As discussed before, marketing to a constituency sometimes involves nothing more than showing those people images of themselves in advertising.

Where the "gay market" might intersect with this theory is in organizations understanding what particular needs gay people have in American society. For example, needs due to the existence of relationships that are committed but not "legal." The provisions gay people have to make to protect our families legally and fiscally, to name just two, are considerable. We cannot play by the same rules as the heterosexual majority because we aren't allowed to. Certainly this seems poised to change, but for now the question is, Can an element of education be focused on acquisition of a market that has these, or other, special needs?

Organizations can and should be looking at the following questions:

- What is orientation?
- What does orientation mean in terms of the decisions people make in their lives?
- How are aspects of finances and legality affected by sexual orientation?
- How are aspects related to various common and ordinary services and products affected by sexual orientation?

- How might characteristics particular to people of a nonheterosexual orientation make them viable customers for that organization?
- Does the necessity for people of a nonheterosexual orientation or minority gender identification to continually "think outside the box" make them viable candidates for our products and services?
- In what ways could we adjust current marketing/sales strategies to specifically target this potential market?
- What new strategies can we come up with to target nonheterosexual people, and what do our people need to know about them in order to leverage these strategies to their fullest?

Based on the answers to these and other important questions, a curriculum for internal sales/marketing training can be developed. What I am talking about here is obviously a targeted marketing scheme, but with a twist. Utilizing principles of diversity education, the organization can be not only proactive or reactive in dealing with internal workplace situations founded in sexual orientation but can be proactive in leveraging the diversity program to create a new market niche if its products, services, or mission lends itself to it. I can think of hundreds of business types that could—from auto makers, to financial services companies, to law firms, to banks, to, well the list is endless indeed.

Chapter 8

DPBs, Civil Unions,
and Same-Sex Marriage

AN IMPORTANT NOTE TO BEGIN

I know I mentioned this when discussing the changing landscape regarding sexual orientation and gender identity in Chapter 1, but there are things happening that I truly never thought I'd see in my lifetime. I actually always believed that there would be a legal recognition for nonheterosexual, monogamous, committed relationships, and that I'd live to see it. However, I really thought it would come too late in my own life for me to want to take advantage of it. My partner and I, like many of our peers, have made provisions for ourselves, each other, and our property as best we can by creating a patchwork of documents, wills, trusts, powers of attorney, joint accounts, and beneficiary arrangements, and in our case, it should all hold up pretty well whether we get married or not.

Not everyone in a gay relationship can say that, because if there are any issues about a person's sexual orientation with members of her or his immediate family—parents or siblings—then nothing they might set up is guaranteed to hold up in court since the law, as it currently stands in the overwhelming majority of the United States, favors next of kin. Parents and siblings, in that order, are next of kin if one doesn't have a legal spouse. This is one of the many, many things that marriage denotes in the United States.

This chapter covers three distinct but interrelated subjects: domestic partner benefits (DPBs), civil unions and registries, and same-sex marriage. I've gone to great pains to discuss each one in terms of how they each stand in January 2005, as I examine the galley of this book, and to also cover every point I raise with my eyes on some sort of a crystal ball that tells me how things may be different by the time the book appears.

I don't know how the same-sex marriage question will be resolved by each of the fifty states, our territories, and the federal government; it can go a number of ways. I don't know how long it's all going to take to wind its way through Congress and fifty legislatures. I don't even know that same-sex marriage or some sort of federally accepted civil-union status is going to make the idea of or necessity for domestic partners disappear. Lots of people don't get married even though they can; it may be a state's right to grant the privilege, but ultimately, it's an individual's right to take advantage of it. Given all the progress that's been made to incorporate partner status in many different kinds of legislation in various states in the United States, and especially given the progress made to include partners in elements of workplace benefits, it seems reasonable to me to think that partners as a recognized unit—gay or straight—will survive even the legalization of same-sex marriage. So everything about DPBs will not necessarily be made immediately moot by gays getting married.

Again, that's only one example of the contingencies that someone must remember when trying to tackle these subjects, either individually or in relation to one another. I've done my best to cover all the bases that I, and those whose research I've depended on, could think of.

DOMESTIC PARTNER BENEFITS

As of the beginning of 2005, about 7,000 organizations have DPBs in place for same-sex couples, and about two-thirds of those have DPBs for heterosexual couples. These companies are of all kinds, of all sizes, and in all the market segments we'd look at, which is to say public entities, including cities and states; private companies, including a majority of the F1000; colleges and universities, including those beholden to state legislatures for funding; and private, nonprofit organizations, unions, and associations. In short, so many that unless a client is benchmarking some aspect of their inclusion practices against their peers, the specific names of who's got what for whom almost never come up. That said, the HRC keeps a very tidy and, I believe, accurate list on their Web site if you really need to know about a particular organization.

San Francisco, Los Angeles, Seattle, Berkeley, Oakland, and the State of California make DPBs, at least for same-sex couples, mandatory for organizations that wish to be contractors to them. New York City and Atlanta are considering similar provisions. Not only have the cities reported cost increases of .02 to 12 percent, but they also report saving money due to lower public health expenditures, because more residents are getting health coverage due to these plans.[1]

Why the explosion in DPBs? It is for two simple reasons. First, the population of people, gay or straight, living in families of their making absent marriage has been steadily increasing for more than fifteen years. The 2000 and 2002 U.S. Census studies gave us counts of how many gay Americans there are (about 15 million self-reported on the 2000 Census and that is probably low by about 10 million or so) and 600,000 gay, self-reported heads of or partners in households with or without children (again, probably low by several millions), and the U.S. Census in 1994 and 1998 had already reported that the number of Americans living in unmarried-partner households had increased at five times the rate of married households. In 1998, 5.9 million people in the United States were living with a partner. Of these, approximately 28 percent, or 1.7 million people, were in same-sex relationships.

The second reason is that almost two decades of data firmly support the notion that DPBs are a low-cost, high-return way to demonstrate inclusion that results in little or no backlash, even from the most fervently discriminatory among us. The plain fact is that study after study unequivocally bears out that upward of 90 percent of Americans believe that if you have a family and you work to support them, you deserve the benefits of that labor. There's also this: The Employee Benefits Research Group found in a survey of 279 HR professionals representing nineteen industries in the United States that DPBs are the number-one recruitment tool for executives and the third-ranked recruitment tool for management and line workers.[2] DPBs were found to be a more effective hiring incentive than telecommuting options, hiring bonuses, stock options, and 401K plans, among other things.

The History of Workplace Benefits

This working generation (anyone from fifteen to eighty years of age) tends to think of employer-provided benefits as a birthright. They aren't, of course, but they may be the closest most people ever get. Benefits as a form of workplace compensation started in the 1940s, when companies who wanted to pay certain employees more were prohibited by law from doing so by way of simple pay increases. So instead of giving the cash directly to the employee, the employer paid for certain products and services such as insurance or housing on the employee's behalf. For those laborers traditionally holding the shorter end of the compensatory stick, workplace benefits derived in part from President Franklin D. Roosevelt's New Deal as a way to subsidize both businesses and employees during and immediately after the Depression.

Since the 1940s, workplace benefits have continued to constitute an integral part of compensation. Even during the boom years of World War II through the development of the suburbs in the 1950s and 1960s, benefits from the workplace were taken for granted. Employers found new and different ways to package benefits, both for the good of employees and to enhance the attractiveness of their workplace over their competitors. Therefore, the idea of benefits constituting a competitive advantage is not new. Organizations have been trying to outdo one another in this fashion for decades.

The economic and symbolic importance of workplace benefits is undeniable. The U.S. Chamber of Commerce released a study stating that between 37 and 40 percent of total employee compensation is comprised of workplace benefits.[3] In concert with these data, 67 percent of respondents to an Employee Benefit Research survey said they would not give up any portion of their employer-provided benefits even in lieu of a higher cash salary. Ironically, the principle that led in part to the creation of such benefits fifty-odd years ago—namely, giving employees benefits in lieu of additional cash salary—is the same one that won't allow employers to back away from this expense now. Obviously this is becoming a very difficult topic in light of the alarming and skyrocketing costs of health insurance in the United States. However, even given the degree of difficulty that organizations are having in keeping their medical/dental plans in place, or having to push more of the cost on the employees, not a single organization has cut DPBs as a cost-saving measure.

Gay or straight, we are all in this particular mess together because we all have the same thing on the line: the ability to provide adequate care to our families. Furthermore, equitable benefits are of vital consequence to gay employees because they represent both recognition of gay relationships and, perhaps more important, they signify equal pay for equal work. In awarding DPBs, the employer is not granting a "new" or "special" benefit to its unmarried, partnered employees. All it is doing is extending existing benefits to another classification of employee based on an expanded set of criteria for eligibility.

The Benefits and How They Work

Workplace benefits are typically viewed as "hard" benefits or "soft" benefits, and it's long been true that many more organizations than have hard DPBs have soft benefits for nonmarried partners and nonlegal dependents of their employees. This includes the federal government, which may allow use of facility privileges, as one example, to family members of employees, which they allow the employees to designate.

Examples of soft benefits are as follows:

- *Private sector:* bereavement leave, sick leave, parenting leave, employee discounts, health and fitness programs, relocation benefits
- *Public sector:* access to school records, registration of partnership, visitation rights in hospitals or prisons, tax benefits for companies in the cities that recognize domestic partners
- *College and university:* child care, faculty/staff privileges, student/faculty housing, university ID privileges, tuition waiver or reimbursement

Examples of hard benefits include the following, regardless of market sector:

- Medical
- Dental
- Pension
- Insurance

Any and all benefits that are offered to legal spouses and dependents of employees can and should be offered to partners within the confines of the applicable tax codes.*

For example, if the organization provides COBRA and FMLA (Family and Medical Leave Act) benefits to families, they should be extended to partners and their dependent children. If the organization pays the proceeds of a private pension plan to legal spouses, but not to dependents, it should make a provision that such benefits would be paid to partners as well. In the case of private pensions, however, the organization under ERISA (Employee Retirement Income Security Act) regulations is under no obligation to make these payments in the event of the untimely death of the employee.

In so far as life insurance is concerned, the organization can allow employee's partners to purchase both life and accidental death/dismemberment through the company if spouses have this option, but there is a tax ramification for this purchase and a tax attorney should be consulted.

In terms of soft benefits, every effort should be made to pointedly include partners in these benefits, in writing and as a matter of company policy, so that there is no uncertainty on the part of any manager or employee as to whether a gay man, for example, may take a day off to attend the funeral of his partner's father. It is very important that there be no ambiguity in company policy about such matters.

Furthermore, if relocation assistance is provided "case by case," as it is in many organizations, relocation assistance for partners being available in this way should also be spelled out.

Should the organization wish to make employee discounts available to partners, it will have to develop a method to track the discounts, due to the tax liability involved.

Medical/Dental Benefits

Although there are no restrictions on partner benefits plans in most jurisdictions and most if not all of the standard insurers and HMO/PPO plans now write them as standard operating procedures, there are still some companies who are not writing them because they choose not to, they have not yet been asked to, or they have simply not

---

* The tax codes are also a moving target these days; an update on that from the second edition will be given later in this chapter.

completed the filings necessary to offer them in all the states where they do business. In the past five years a startling change has occurred: it is now more difficult to find an insurance provider who won't write these benefits than it is to find those who will.

Only one jurisdiction (Virginia) is left in which insurance regulations preclude standard insurers from writing these plans. These rules almost never apply to HMOs/PPOs and never apply at all to self-insured plans. There are always ways around this situation, either by limiting the kinds of plans offered in a place like Virginia or where some of the organization's providers have declined to participate, or by licensing the plan in another state where the business operates.

Pension Plans

The employer will pay the vested portion of a deceased employee's pension to a legal spouse. It can, if it chooses, also pay any vested monies to a partner. However, under ERISA, if the pension is fully company funded, it need not pay these benefits to the surviving partner.

In the case of a 401(K), the employee can name as beneficiary any person with an "insurable interest." This is not affected in any way by the implementation of a DPB plan.

Either the employee/retiree or the partner would claim the pension payments as income for tax purposes unless there is a tax-qualified status to the plan or to their resolution of the monies when paid. There is no imputed calculation for the employer either way.

Term Life Insurance

Although employees can buy term life insurance for their spouses, they cannot for partners. A nonlegal spouse cannot be party to group life insurance unless the employee pays the entire premium. This is due to the tax status of insurance premiums (life and disability).

A partner or any person who can show an insurable interest can, of course, be the beneficiary of a life insurance policy of her or his partner. The proceeds of such policies are taxed as income (depending on estate maneuvers and so on) and are not the calculation responsibility of the employer.

Employee Stock Ownership

If the corporation allows vested stock to become the property of a legal spouse in the case of death of the employee, then it has the option (as with pension plans) to award that stock to a domestic partner.

Disability Plans

All employees, regardless of family type or marital status, have equal access to the benefits of long- and/or short-term disability insurance. Legal spouses or legal dependents have no additional rights or access under these plans. Therefore, they would not likely apply to a DPB plan.

Adoption Assistance

Only two states, Florida and New Hampshire, specifically do not allow joint adoptions by lesbian and gay couples. The rest of the United States either allows them outright or allows them due to precedent-setting cases in those states, or allows them through a method by which first a gay couple adopts through a single parent, and then the second parent adopts the child or children in question. Therefore, in most of the United States, adoption assistance likely applies to DPB plans. There is likely an imputed value to monies provided for this purpose similar to that in relocation assistance plans. This tax burden is shared by any employee who accepts such monetary assistance, regardless of marital status. However, there may be tax breaks for people who adopt (again, regardless of gender, sexual orientation, or marital status); either way, the monies should be treated as taxable income to the employee.

Dependent Care Referral

Because this is a referral service available to "families" and there is no imputed/cash value for it, there would seem to be no reason why it could not be accessed by/for partners and nondependent children of the employee.

Health Care and Dependent Care Spending Accounts

Deductions for dependent care are designed to be made pretax in order to help the employee put money aside for dependent care and to do so while reducing the income-tax burden. However, due to federal tax code, benefits for persons who are not the legal spouse or legal dependent of an employee cannot be provided for pretax. Therefore, there is no benefit for an employee with a nonlegal spouse or nonlegal dependent to provide for those persons in that manner. A private investment plan (or second-parent adoption) would/might be more advantageous arrangements.

The organization does have the option to make the plan available in its DPB plans on an after-tax basis and let employees calculate what option is to their fiscal advantage.

Educational Assistance for Children

If the corporation's policy calls for such assistance to be provided only to legal dependents, then the employee's nonlegal dependent children (i.e., does the employee provide for 51 percent of the minor's care and claim the minor as a deduction for tax purposes?) would not qualify for such assistance. The corporation has an option to change the qualifying requirements for such assistance. The value of such assistance would be imputed income unless other tax-qualifying events supercede. Please consult a tax advisor for the status of monies for education.

Employee Discounts

Employee discounts have an imputed value that require a separate tracking system, and so although more organizations are offering them to partners, typically the employee has to make the purchase because no elegant solution to track the imputed value of a product discount, especially in retail, yet exists.

Bereavement Leave

This is a "soft benefit" that should be awarded to employees, regardless of gender or sexual orientation, so that they can observe the passing of a loved one who is technically not a family member (by marriage) but who is in reality a family member due to the partner relationship. There is no monetary value to this benefit. It should be awarded in the same manner that employees are entitled to attend to family/in-law matters in cases of marital family relationships and responsibilities. It should also be afforded in cases involving nonlegal dependents of the employee who may be legal dependents of the partner or who may only be in custody of the partner (as in adoption or foster-care arrangements, or while custody due to divorce is being worked out. This last is occurring more often as more people who got married for the sake of convention are coming out of the closet to live their lives in the open).

FMLA-Like Leaves and COBRA-Like Arrangements

Although the federal acts that initiate these plans do not specifically include nonlegal spouses or dependents, they do not exclude them either (for nonfederal employees outside the auspices of the Office of Personal Management). Therefore, most organizations with DPB plans make FMLA-like arrangements with employees who are not married or whose dependents are not legal to allow unpaid leave for the twelve-month period with the assurance of job retention, and so on. Most, if not all, also extend COBRA-like benefits to partners of employees who qualify for COBRA upon discontinuation of their employment.

No imputed values exist for either of these. FMLA benefits do not affect income (except possibly to reduce taxable income when elected), and COBRA requires the payment of premiums in their entirety by the employee/partner with no monetary contribution from the employer after separation.

Employee Assistance Programs

In most employee assistance programs (EAPs), it is left to the discretion of the employee to define "family" as he or she sees fit. Because the purpose of an EAP is to provide support to an employee who may have problems involving family, it is usually deemed proper and necessary that the employee be able to assess those individuals who positively or negatively affect his or her life and/or job performance. Therefore, partners are well advised to be included in that group with access to the EAP suite of services.

Relocation Benefits

It is unreasonable of an employer to acknowledge sexual orientation and DPBs without including equitable relocation policies for partners. In almost all cases in the private sector in which relocation expenses are reimbursed for spouses, they are also reimbursed for partners (including for house-hunting trips, and so on). The value of such assistance would be imputed income unless other tax-qualifying events supercede. Please consult a tax advisor for the status of monies relative to relocation.

The Cost of Domestic Partner Benefits

There are three questions that most often arise during any discussion of DPBs.

- How many people will elect the benefits?
- How much will it cost the organization?
- What are the tax ramifications?

Enrollment Realities

The first factor that determines how much a plan will cost is how many employees will elect it. Average enrollment in any organization offering these benefits remains at less than 3 percent of the total employee population. The organization can further control enrollment by purposefully limiting the benefits to same-sex partners and their children only.

Common Ground's study, undertaken in 2000 to 2001, revealed that the average enrollment in plans for which the total eligible population is between 1,000 and 100,000 is 0.7 percent to 1 percent in gay-only plans and 2 percent to 4 percent in gay-and-straight plans. Only in plans for which less than 1,000 or more than 100,000 people are eligible do the "take rates" in gay-only plans exceed 1 percent or exceed 5 percent in gay-and-straight plans. A younger-than-average workforce (i.e., a workforce whose average age is 25 or less), may experience higher enrollment numbers for (primarily) its heterosexual members.

The question is often asked, "Why do straight couples elect the benefits more often than gay couples do?" The most obvious reason is that there are simply more straight people in the world, at least a three to one ratio, if not a little more. But there are other reasons.

1. In many straight relationships, married or not, one partner performs the more traditional role of housewife or househusband and caretaker (whether there are kids are not). This makes it easier for the employee's partner to qualify for DPBs because the partner's employment status is a big part of the qualification process.
2. In gay relationships, two things are common: first, both adult partners work and have benefits through their own employers; and second, because of the tax ramifications of DPBs, even if one partner's plan is "better" than the other's, the imputed value of DPBs would keep a partner from accepting that cost as compared to his or her own, free or less expensive (out of pocket), plan.
3. As a continuation of point two, many organizations will not let a person—spouse, partner, or otherwise—join their benefits plan if the person has his or her own.
4. Fear of revealing one's orientation is another thing that keeps enrollment—specifically gay enrollment—down. Frankly, even when confidentiality is promised, fear of being "outed" by the process of electing benefits remains a big problem for many gay people. This is why it is of enormous importance that DPBs not be introduced in a vacuum where no preparations have been made to help members of the organization deal with their issues—pro and con—regarding not only the DPBs themselves but also the inexorably connected questions related to sexual orientation and the acknowledgment of same in work/family programs.

About Adverse Selection

Contrary to warnings and predictions made by insurance companies and other concerned parties since the mid-1980s, extending coverage to partners—specifically gay male partners—has not resulted in increased costs due to "adverse selection," which is a polite term for HIV/AIDS-affected parties.

In no instance in which a surcharge was demanded by an insurance carrier or HMO at the start of same-sex partner plans was that surcharge still in force two years later; such surcharges are unheard of today.

Another fact about DPB plans that not only keeps their cost down but also contributes to lowering premiums for everyone is that people in partner situations tend to be younger, and younger people tend to be healthier. This means that a healthier population is brought into the group plan, which helps drive premium costs down for everyone. As straight people age, they are more likely to marry, and so their effect on the cost of the plans lessens; and soon, this will also be true for gay partners in the plan who will opt for marriage or legal partnership, however that shakes out. For now, however, these people represent a cost savings for everyone.

In order of cost to health plans, HIV/AIDS ranks fifth behind maternity, heart disease, cancer, and Alzheimer's disease. There has not been a single case of spiking in a plan's cost due to AIDS anywhere in the United States.

The Cost of DPBs Related to Taxes

Costs for Employers

Employers treat their premium contribution to the domestic partner's coverage as a compensation expense under IRS Code Section 162 attributable to the employment of the "employee partner." In other words, they treat it just as they treat premium contributions for legal spouses and dependents. Employers therefore take these premium contributions as tax deductions by classifying them as an "ordinary and necessary business expense."

These actions, to date, are based on Private Letter Rulings, (PLRs) issued to organizations by the IRS to employers who have asked for them. A PLR does not, by definition, constitute a precedent, and so a tax attorney should always be consulted, but absent any sweeping rulings to date by the IRS, organizations with DPBs are operating in this manner.

In those cases in which employee benefits premiums are paid from VEBA (Voluntary Employee Benefit Association) Trust accounts, a separate account must be created to pay for nonlegal spouse and dependent benefits. Doing so does not affect the tax status of the payments to the organization.

Costs for Employees

The tax picture for employees who elect coverage for their partners is still not as favorable as it is to employers for whom it's mostly a nonissue. However, there are some significant changes to available information that I can provide in this edition.

There are two rules of thumb regarding the imputed (taxable) value of DPBs when provided for a nonlegal spouse or dependent. One is that the employee's contribution to the plan on behalf of the partner/nondependent children must be made after taxes. The other is that the fair market value of the benefits for these partners and/or their children must be added to the employees' amount of taxable income for the year.

The important tax code in the discussion of DPBs is Section 152, which, in general terms, specifies who is a dependent for the purposes of assessing taxes. If a recipient of a benefit is a legal spouse or dependent, the fair market value of the benefit is considered tax qualified (no taxes assessed). Keep this in mind as you read further.

What Is Fair Market Value?

The amount of a benefit that is taxable (imputed) is called its fair market value (FMV). Most organizations determine this value by doing a calculation of the full, unsubsidized individual rate for insurance, less the remainder of the employee's family rate minus the employee's individual rate. In other words, the value is the amount of premium paid by the employer toward the partner's coverage minus whatever the employee contributes toward that coverage. Some organizations still calculate the FMV by taking the COBRA rate for the employee only, less a 2 percent administration fee. In truth, doing it this way never was advantageous to the employee when compared to the first way of doing the calculation, and it's even less advantageous now, when health insurance premiums are so much more expensive.

The following examples demonstrate the current (typical) calculation of fair market value and the after-tax responsibility of the employee to the plan for his or her partner and/or his or her partner's dependents:

	Health	Dental	Vision	Total
Employee	$126	$43.09	$7.05	$176.14
Employee+1	$398	$82.30	$15.23	$496.03
Employee+Family	$461	$128.23	$15.73	$604.96
Employee+Children	$334	$128.23	$15.73	$477.96

Situation One

You have coverage for yourself and you add a domestic partner.

$496.03 × 20% = employee contribution of $99.20
$176.14 × 20% = employee contribution for himself or herself of $35.23
$99.20 – $35.23 = $63.97 is paid for partner after tax

Imputed income:
Employer contribution for two people is $496.03 × 80% = $396.82.
Employer contribution for employee only is $176.14 × 80% = $140.91.
$396.82 – $140.91 – employee's contribution for himself or herself of $35.23 = $220.68 is imputed value per pay period. This number is added to the employee's gross for the period and taxed accordingly. It can be listed as a separate line item if you wish. The result will be the same.

Situation Two

You have coverage for yourself and you add your partner and your partner's child.

$604.96 × 20% = employee contribution of $120.99

$120.99 – employee's contribution for herself or himself of $35.23 = $85.76

$85.76 ÷ 3 (or whatever number of children added) for the employee, the partner, and the child = $28.58

$28.58 × 2 (for partner and child) = $57.17. Amount paid after tax by the employee with $63.81 paid pretax

Imputed income:

$604.96 × 80% = employer contribution for family of $483.97

Employer's contribution for the employee herself or himself = $140.91

$483.97 – $140.91 = $343.06 is the amount added to the employee's gross for the period and taxed accordingly.

Situation Three

You have coverage for yourself and you add your partner's child only (for the sake of the exercise, we will assume one child that the partner cannot provide coverage for).

$477.96 × 20% = employee's contribution of $95.59

$95.59 – employee's contribution for himself or herself of $35.23 = $60.36

$60.36 is paid for child after tax

Imputed income:

$477.96 × 80% for employer's contribution = $382.37

Employer's contribution for employee is $140.91

$382.37 – $140.91 = $241.46 is the amount added to the employee's gross for the period and taxed accordingly.

Two Very Important New Facts
About the Tax Discussion

1. Section 152 of the tax code (which, as I told you previously, is the most important one when it comes to taxes and DPBs for employees) specifies who is a dependent for tax purposes.* Before Item 9 of Section 152 is the word "or," which means (according to some tax people) that even if a person (the nonemployee partner in this case) doesn't meet the legal definition of a tax dependent per Section 152 Items 1-8, he or she may meet the legal definition of dependent if he or she receives more than half of his or her support from your employee and he or she is a member of your employee's household. This is true even if the employee does not claim the partner as a tax dependent because the nonemployee partner has an income of more than $2500.00 per year (which means he or she must file his or her own return). Many organizations are allowing their employees to designate their partners and their partner's children as members of the employee's household so as not to have to pay the partners'/dependents' premiums after tax and so as not to have to assess tax on the FMV of the benefits. I strongly recommend that you explore your options with your tax advisors. Also, be sure to keep in mind that if an employee, or anyone, in the United States lies about income or dependents or anything else when filing taxes, it is the individual who is responsible; the employer is not responsible, as it can only act in concert with what the employee says is true.

2. The second thing that is really important relative to DPBs and the whole taxation issue is a bill in Congress called the Domestic

---

*The term *dependent* in this context means any of the following individuals more than half of whose support, for the calendar year in which the taxable year of the taxpayer begins, was received from the taxpayer or is treated under subsection "c" or "e" as received from the taxpayer.

1. a son or daughter of the taxpayer, or a descendant of either
2. a stepson or stepdaughter of the taxpayer
3. a brother, sister, stepbrother, or stepsister of the taxpayer
4. the father or mother of the taxpayer, or an ancestor of either
5. a stepfather or stepmother of the taxpayer
6. a son or daughter of a brother or sister of the taxpayer
7. a brother or sister of the father or mother of the taxpayer
8. a son-in-law, daughter-in-law, father-in-law, mother-in-law, brother-in-law, or sister-in-law of the taxpayer

   or

9. an individual (other than the individual who at any time during the taxable year was the spouse, determined without regard to section 7703 [former Code section 143] of the taxpayer) who, for the taxable year of the taxpayer, has as his or her principal place of abode the home of the taxpayer and is a member of the taxpayer's household.

Partner Health Benefits Equity Act of 2003 (HR 935 and S. 1702), a.k.a. the Tax Equity Health Plan Beneficiaries Act (House version), that would effectively rewrite the IRS code of 1986 to end the taxation of partners altogether. As of January 2005, this bill continues to bounce around Congress since its introduction in late 2003. As this book goes to press, it remains to be seen how the federal government will treat the tax ramifications of same-sex marriages that are legal in Massachusetts but remain invalidated by the federal government or the IRS. One thing is certain though: Congress should pass the DP Health Benefits Equity Act of 2003 in order to afford all people some tax relief due them in light of their legal marriages in the Commonwealth of Massachusetts. The continued delay is unacceptable.

Definition of a Domestic Partner Based on Current Best Practices

- Your domestic partner is the same sex as you (this for same-sex only plans).
- You are both at least age eighteen and mentally competent to consent to a contract.
- You are responsible for each other's financial welfare.
- You acknowledge responsibility for each other's general welfare.
- You have lived together for at least six months and have not had another person enrolled as a domestic partner under this organization's benefits program in the past six months immediately preceding your current application or partner designation.
- You are presently not legally married to anyone.
- You are life partners and would get legally married should the option become available. In the interim, would apply for civil union status should that option become available in your home state or commonwealth.
- You are registered as domestic partners if there is a local domestic partner registry in your town, city, or state (a list of these is available).
- You are not related in such a way as to prohibit legal marriage should that option become available (prohibitions do, and may, vary from state to state).

- Your domestic partner is not eligible for Medicare, nor is he or she eligible (as an employee or retiree) for coverage under this organization's benefit plan(s).
- You agree to inform the company in the event that the domestic partnership terminates.

Some Related Decisions to Make

Once the organization has set upon its definition of what constitutes a partner using this standard or some other, it must decide whether an affidavit of partnership will be required, whether a time requirement will be stipulated, whether it will also require marriage licenses from heterosexual employees, whether termination affidavits will be required, and under what circumstances another partner could be added to a DPB plan after the termination of a partnership. Last, it must decide whether to include straight couples in the plan.

Whether both straight and gay people are included in these definitions is entirely up to the organization. The consequences of this decision will be seen, as stated before, in the "take rates" for the benefits, but again, unless the organization employs less than 1,000 people or more than 100,000, the differences are negligible.

If the organization's nondiscrimination policy makes reference to "sexual orientation" (we all have one), "gender," "marital status," "compensation," and/or "benefits," it may be well advised to be as inclusive as possible. Frankly, there are thousands of organizations whose nondiscrimination statements say all of these things and they still don't have partner benefits. These thousands are operating in violation of their own policies and ought to take a close look at that.

Miscellaneous Details

Fraud

There has not been a single documented case of fraud perpetrated by a person or partnership (gay or straight) in any DPB plan in the United States since 1982. All fraud in benefits plans appears to be committed by people claiming to be legally married who are not. Affidavits of partnership make it very difficult and very unwise to elect DPBs for which the parties do not qualify.

Termination of Benefits

In almost all cases of partnership termination, the employee is required to notify the employer in writing. In some cases (and this is recommended for the protection of the nonemployee partner) an affidavit of termination will be signed by both parties. Common Ground recommends the use of a termination affidavit even in those situations in which an affidavit of partnership is not required.

It is not unusual for an employee who terminates a domestic partnership to have to wait three months, six months, or even a year before enrolling a new partner. This is in contrast to heterosexual married people who can, if they wish, divorce and remarry in time frames, in most cases, much shorter than these. Whether to require a "buffer" between the termination of one partnership and the establishment of another for the purposes of benefits is up to the employer.

The termination agreement need not be very complex or convoluted. It should simply assert that the partnership has ended (whether the ending is amicable is not the point) and that the partner understands that his or her health/dental insurance and status as beneficiary of other DPB plan provisions will end as of a given date. It is not unusual for a COBRA-like extension of up to ninety days to be offered the partner in order to give him or her time to secure other insurance.

Sample Affidavit

We, (employee's name) and (partner's name), certify that we are domestic partners as described in the benefits enrollment material of (organization name), and that we are therefore eligible for benefits. (Note: If you have a Certificate of Domestic Partnership from a city or municipality authorized to grant same, no other proof shall be necessary. If not, the employer and/or its agents or insurers reserve the right to request proof[s] of the nature described in our domestic partner policy as relates to the definition of a domestic partner. These proofs typically consist of mortgage/rent receipts for at least the term of relationship required, joint bank account statements, designation of beneficiary on wills, insurance policies, investment holdings, etc.)

1. We have an exclusive, committed relationship and we have been in such a relationship for at least six months. (Author

note: this could be one month or twelve months. There is no fixed time frame, nor is a time frame always stipulated.)

1a. We are of the same sex. (This is included only if that is a stipulation.)

2. We are responsible for each other's common welfare and financial obligations. We are liable to third parties for any obligations incurred by each other and will continue to be so liable during the period that the nonemployee partner is covered by the benefits program.

3. We share the same principal place of residence and intend to do so indefinitely.

4. We are at least eighteen years old and are both mentally competent to consent and enter into a contract.

5. Neither of us is legally married to anyone else, nor has had another domestic partner within the past one (six, eight, etc.) month(s).

6. We are not related by blood to a degree of closeness that would prohibit legal marriage in the state in which we legally reside.

7. We agree to notify the employer if our partnership status changes to such a degree that the nonemployee partner would no longer be entitled to benefits under the plan definition. We agree to notify the company in writing within one month (31 days) of such a change.

8. If such termination of relationship occurs, the employee partner agrees that he/she will not file a subsequent Affidavit of Domestic Partnership for a period of _____ months from the date of notification in writing of the existing partnership's termination unless the Affidavit is filed for the same nonemployee partner.

9. We understand that (the employer) is not liable or forced to extend COBRA to the nonemployee partner, but does so by its own choice.

10. We understand and agree that the employee partner can and will make health plan elections on behalf of the nonemployee partner.

11. We understand that under applicable state and federal tax laws, employer contributions for the nonemployee partner's health benefits can result in additional imputed income to the

employee and that such tax may not be paid with pretax dollars. We understand that it is our responsibility to determine our tax liabilities.

12. We understand that any fraudulent claims of partnership, or any failure to comply with the requirements for plan qualification can result in loss of employment and/or civil action against us to recover losses, fees, premiums, and so on.

13. We understand that some courts recognize nonmarriage relationships, not limited to opposite-sex, common-law relationships or opposite-sex domestic partnerships, as the equivalent of legal marriage in terms of establishing and dividing community property.

14. We understand that this document is filed confidentially but may be subject to subpoena.

We have read and we understand the terms and conditions under which this coverage is offered and accepted. We declare that all statements assigned by us are true and that any or all documents submitted to support these statements, if requested, are also true and verifiable.

Signatures and dates. (Notarization is an option.)

Sample Termination Agreement

The employee (fill in name) and his/her domestic partner (fill in name) hereby mutually attest to the dissolution of their partnership, said partnership having made the nonemployee partner eligible for domestic partner benefits from (fill in organization name).

The nonemployee partner hereby relinquishes his/her eligibility for domestic partner benefits effective (fill in date).

The nonemployee partner hereby requests/does not request COBRA-like benefits to commence on (fill in date) for the specified allowable time period.

The nonemployee partner can be reached at: (fill in complete address, e-mail address, and phone and fax numbers as applicable) for the purposes of setting up the COBRA account and/or for a copy of this organization-executed Termination Agreement of Domestic Partner Benefits.

Signed and dated (by the employee)

Signed and dated (by the nonemployee partner)

Notarized
Signed and dated by an organizational representative

Implementation FAQ

Q: How should we communicate that we are going to offer DPBs to our employees?

A: Typically DPBs are rolled out in conjunction with the next open enrollment period. The organizations that I've worked with who have handled the rollout most successfully have included a "kit" that contains all the necessary forms to enroll, an explanation of the tax implications, and a rundown of what benefits are included in the plan and why. They also explain if any benefits are not included in the plan. Beyond this, a good DPB implementation kit will proactively answer questions before they are asked. The questions (and answers for same) I'd recommend including in the kit are as follows:

- Why is the organization offering DPBs?
- Why are there tax implications for these benefits?
- Why are we offering these benefits to same-sex couples only? (if it applies).
- Do I put my employment at risk if I elect these benefits?
- What constitutes a partner for the purposes of these benefits?
- By offering these DPBs, are fewer benefits available for traditional families?
- Aren't these benefits going to cost the organization too much?
- Do all or most of our health providers allow this?
- Can I name my partner as a beneficiary under the basic term life insurance, 401(K), and pension plans? (as they apply).
- Are there forms I need to fill out, and is there a deadline to get them in?
- What happens if we don't meet the partner eligibility rules now but will in the middle of the year? Do we have to wait for the next open enrollment?

The Big Question for the Period of Transition

Ever since January 2004 when the Massachusetts Supreme Court released its decision that gay people could start getting married in that commonwealth in May 2004 (which they did), I've been asked one question more than any other: Should an organization make the decision to implement domestic partner benefits based on current (January 2005) access to civil unions and same-sex marriage or should it wait and see what happens down the road?

My answer is that I don't think that an organization should wait to implement DPBs if they are inclined to investigate offering them because although the status of same-sex marriage in all fifty of the United States will have an effect on whether there will be DPBs in the future, right now the reasons for offering DPBs, especially to same-sex couples, are as valid as they were ten years ago. That is, for people who want these benefits, it's about equal pay for equal work, and the ability to adequately provide for and protect their families.

As I said at the beginning of this chapter, I think that there is a good chance that even same-sex marriage's legalization will not necessarily make the classification of partners disappear, and even if it does, it is all going to take years to fully shake out. There is no reason to wait.

CIVIL UNIONS

> We hold that the State is constitutionally required to extend to same-sex couples the common benefits and protections that flow from marriage under Vermont law. The extension of the Common Benefits Clause (of the Vermont State Constitution) to acknowledge the plaintiffs as Vermonters who seek nothing more, nor less, than legal protection and security for their avowed commitment to an intimate and lasting human relationship is simply, when all is said and done, a recognition of our common humanity.

> From the decision of the Vermont Supreme Court, December 1999, mandating that the Vermont State Legislature would extend to lesbian and gay couples the same rights, protections, benefits, and obligations available to nongay couples through marriage

With this ruling in the spring of 2000, Vermont became the only state or commonwealth in the United States to legally recognize same-sex couples by granting civil unions. In that year, Vermont began allowing same-sex couples to form civil unions, making them eligible for the 300-plus state benefits available to married couples. The federal government does not recognize these unions, nor do they confer any of the 1,049 federal rights and responsibilities of legal marriage.

People from other states can go to Vermont and register their union, but their union will not be recognized by their home state and they will not be entitled or responsible for the rights and responsibilities that their state confers upon married people.

If a company that doesn't have partner benefits as a matter of policy across the board has operations in Vermont and employees in Vermont who have registered for a civil union, then they must offer partner benefits to the partner of their employee. The Commonwealth of Vermont will not tax these benefits, but the federal government will.

OTHER PROVISIONS SHORT
OF CIVIL UNIONS OR LEGAL MARRIAGE

Two states, Hawaii (Reciprocal Beneficiaries Act) and California (Domestic Partner Registry Act), have made provisions for same-sex partners that offer some, but not all, of the rights and responsibilities offered married people in those states and don't go as far even as Vermont's civil unions. Fifty-six or so cities and municipalities offer registries for partners and may extend things such as rights to hospital and jail visitation, child care leave, and some parental rights to people who register in those jurisdictions.

California's inclusive policies go further than any other state. They include but aren't limited to the ability to do the following:

- Make medical treatment decisions on behalf of a partner who can't.
- Use sick leave to care for a child, stepchild, parent, domestic partner, or child of the partner.
- Adopt the child of a domestic partner using existing procedures for stepchild adoption.

- Receive the same state tax exemption for health care costs that is provided to spouses/dependents.
- Sue for infliction of emotional distress and wrongful death if their domestic partner is killed due to negligence.
- Receive unemployment benefits if the partner is transferred by his or her company to a location not commutable.
- File disability benefits on behalf of an incapacitated partner.

New Jersey, on January 7, 2004, became the third state to have a domestic partner bill that affords residents of that state with certain survivor rights, hospital visitation, and control of each other's medical decisions. Domestic partners of state employees are now entitled to workplace benefits, and state insurance companies will be obligated to make partner coverage available to private companies as well who wish to offer them.

WHY SAME-SEX MARRIAGE IS INEVITABLE

In the second edition of this book, I quoted statistics from a *Wall Street Journal*/NBC News poll indicating that 75 percent of Americans, like it or not, believed that same-sex marriage would be legal in at least one state by 2005. Seventy-five percent of Americans turned out to be correct. As much as same-sex marriage was made a matter of morality in the 2004 elections, a clear plurality of Americans favor same-sex marriage. Statistically, it's about 49 percent yes and 49 percent no as of January 2005. However, a clear majority of Americans favor civil union status for same-sex couples with all the rights and responsibilities of marriage. In addition, it's important to remember that the percentage of Americans who are against same-sex marriage is less than the percentage that still opposed interracial marriage when the Supreme Court struck down prohibitions against those marriages.[4]

For some, it's the word *marriage* that is the problem, and they believe that if gay people were to get all of the same rights and responsibilities as civil marriage, only it was called civil union, they would be satisfied. To me this is still back-of-the-bus, separate-but-equal thinking, and there is no such thing as separate but equal. Beyond that, the word "marriage" does matter, because it implies that there is a bond, a commitment that goes beyond any other type between the two people involved. It requires love, trust, respect, honesty, commitment, fidelity—all of those things are wrapped up in that word.

Therefore, I predict that, even if this country does go first for "civil unions" which are equitable in every sense of the word to marriage, millions of gay people will both accept it and continue to fight for the full legitimacy of their relationships by having them referred to not as "unions" but as "marriages."

WHAT'S AT STAKE IN MARITAL STATUS

In the past three years, while this issue of civil unions/same-sex marriage has been coming up more frequently and seriously, I have not encountered a single married heterosexual who knew about the number and scope of their federal and state obligations under the marriage laws. This is almost as sad as the fact that less than 30 percent of voting-eligible adults bother to vote. It's infuriating to those who can't marry, because the blockage to same-sex marriage is perpetrated mostly by people who don't have the faintest idea what they are talking about in the first place. It is another of life's unfunny ironies. However, absent the ability to get married, people in thoughtful, committed relationships must, and certainly often (but not always) do, go out of their way to make provisions to protect the relationship legally, financially, and in terms of their fiduciary responsibility to each other.

These things are wills, powers of attorney, health care proxies, living wills, bank or other joint financial accounts, trusts, and joint deeds of property ownership. All of these are also duplicated by some married couples, but the majority of what is specifically covered in all of them is implied by the civil marriage contract unless other arrangements are specifically arranged by the parties. This goes to the point that you can, in a legal marriage, release yourself and/or your spouse from any number of his or her legal, financial, fiduciary, or even residence responsibilities to you and still remain legally married. Partners cannot do any of that.

In fact, 1,049 federal rights and responsibilities are tied to legal marriage, and each state confers upon its married citizens another 150 to 300 beyond those. Some of these, most of these in fact, are things that partners cannot, under any circumstances, replicate for the protection of themselves or their partners, no matter how much money they spend or who their lawyer is. These include the following:

- Automatic assumption of spouse's pension (including IRAs, ROTHs, 401[K])
- Automatic inheritance, including associated tax breaks and access to gift-tax relief
- Automatic housing lease transfer
- Bereavement leave
- Burial determination
- Certain property rights
- Child custody
- Crime victim's recovery benefits
- Domestic violence protection
- Exemption from property tax on partner's death
- Immunity from testifying against partner in legal matters
- Insurance breaks (property, life, disability)
- Joint adoption (except in New Jersey as of January 1, 2000) and foster care
- Joint bankruptcy
- Joint parenting
- Reduced-rate memberships
- Sick leave to care for partner
- Visitation of partner's children
- Visitation of partner in hospital or prison
- Wrongful death (loss of consort) benefits
- Social Security benefits

This is only a partial list, and it admittedly leaves out some of the "downside" to legal marriage, such as the so-called marriage penalty tax (which is being phased out by Congress—just in time, perhaps, for gay people not to be burdened by it—this would be another example of one of life's funny ironies). Why do people get married? Usually for love and occasionally for less noble reasons. What does their marriage mean? Typically much more than they ever imagined.

WHERE SAME-SEX MARRIAGE STANDS NOW

Currently, a federal Defense of Marriage Act (DOMA) generally limits marriage to one man/one woman (at a time). Also, more than thirty states in the United States have similar DOMA statutes on the books. The constitutionality of these laws has not yet been challenged (as of January 2005) only because there was no basis upon which to challenge them. That base is beginning to solidify on the foundation of the same-sex marriages being performed in Massachusetts. DOMA laws will (eventually) be challenged on grounds that Congress violated its constitutional enumerated duties by instituting a federal marriage act when marriage is a state's right, on the basis of violating the Equal Protection Clause of the Fourteenth Amendment, or both. Or perhaps the very clever lawyers at GLAD (Gay & Lesbian Advocates & Defenders) will think of another strategy. It was they, after all, who won equitable marriage rights for gay people in Massachusetts.

At least in the beginning of all this, it seems certain that the federal government will not recognize same-sex marriages in Massachusetts, California, and wherever else they are being performed just as it has never recognized Vermont's civil unions. Aside from the federal implications, no state has a residency requirement for marriage. So licenses issued by Massachusetts would have to be recognized by the other states because the full-faith and credit provision of the U.S. Constitution guarantees that licenses issued by one state will be honored by the others. Naturally, we can expect some states and the federal government to put up quite a fuss about recognizing these marriage licenses.

Obviously, the federal courts, and most likely the U.S. Supreme Court, will get involved in due time. However, no matter how fast the courts at state or federal levels act, there will be a time when thousands of people and their employers will find themselves in an uncomfortable and confrontational limbo. In fact, since more than 4,000 couples got married in San Francisco in the spring of 2004, that time has essentially already happened.

WHY SAME-SEX MARRIAGE MEANS BUSINESS

Whatever your personal opinion about same-sex marriage, civil unions, or other related matters of family life in the United States, if you are a human resources professional, corporate counsel, or employment law/policy consultant, the status of same-sex relationships is vitally important to you. As a professional charged with ensuring that your organization's policies and actions fall within the realm of either law or common practice, it is important to understand the salient issues of legal same-sex relationships so that you can make informed decisions or recommendations.

This Q&A addresses what employers of all kinds, whether they currently offer domestic partner benefits or not, can expect to deal with when their gay employees get married.

Q: If an employee brings you a marriage license for a same-sex marriage, how do you treat that employee and his or her spouse for tax purposes if you are currently offering domestic partner benefits and taxing them as nonlegal dependents?

A: There are three ways that state tax laws are structured in the United States.

- State filing status is tied to federal filing status, whether the state has any marriage restrictions or not.
- State filing status is not tied to federal filing status, but there is a state DOMA law.
- State filing status is not tied to federal status and there is not a state DOMA law.

In the first two cases, the employer will be obligated to follow state and federal law while the marital status of employees is being sorted out in the courts. Because of that, employers will still feel they have to assess the partner's portion of premium to be paid by the employee after tax and that the fair market value of the benefits be counted as imputed (taxable) income.

However, employees are going to insist that they are legally married as soon as they get a license and have a wedding of any kind, and they will bring great pressure to bear upon their employers not to take the premiums after tax or to assess the tax penalty on their W-2. If your employees do this and refuse to pay for their spouses'/partners' benefits under the old domestic partner benefits rules, you may as an employer ask the IRS for a private letter ruling. You'll most likely be told that they are not legal dependents/spouses and that the old rules apply. Therefore, if your employee insists on being treated as a legally married person, you will probably have to do so and keep a strict separate accounting of how their benefits are being provided and paid for until such time as the legal aspects of same-sex marriage work their way out.

I mentioned earlier in this chapter, an act is pending in Congress, currently in the Senate Finance Committee, called the domestic Partner Health Benefits Equity Act in the Senate (S. 1702) and the Tax Equity for Health Plan Beneficiaries Act in the House (HR 935). This act would do away with the inequities in the current tax code that make partner benefits payable only with after-tax dollars and would end the imputed value of these benefits. Employers should contact their representatives and senators and insist upon passage of these acts as quickly as possible. Not only because it's the right thing to do in terms of tax equity but also because it will defuse the immediate situation for gay employees with hard (medical/dental) benefits for the short term.

Q: If an employee brings you a marriage license for a same-sex marriage and your organization currently does not offer domestic partner benefits, does any of this concern you?

A: Yes, it most definitely does, because it's not only your organization-offered benefits (hard and/or soft) that are involved. There are other things involved that fall under state or federal marriage status in the way that they are offered. One example is the Family and Medical Leave Act (FMLA); another example has to do with pension plans: private or 401(K) types.

Gay people who work for you and get married in any jurisdiction that offers it will insist that their partners/spouses be treated exactly as heterosexual married employees are for these and a whole slew of other benefits or program requirements, from tuition assistance to use of facilities to pretax flexible spending accounts. Evidence of this can already be seen. Consider the case as written up by the Associated Press on February 22, 2004,[5] in which a couple asked State Farm Insurance company for the marriage-discount rate on their car insurance after having gotten married in San Francisco. First the company said it would honor the discount, and then it changed its mind. State Farm can expect to end up in court over this and whether it wins or loses is hardly the point. The point is, lots of companies are about to find themselves on the wrong side of these sorts of lawsuits.

Q: If some of your gay employees go to Massachusetts and get married there, will you have to acknowledge that marriage, and what

will that mean absent your state or the federal government not acknowledging these marriages in the short and/or long term?

A: All employers are obligated to follow the laws in the jurisdictions in which they operate. It does get confusing when the laws in
one place differ dramatically from the laws in others where a company does business, but same-sex marriage is hardly the only type of
situation that brings this to bear. The problem for employers is that
same-sex marriage is an issue that, unlike other sorts of prohibitions,
does tend to affect people at a baser, more emotional level, whether
you are gay and want to marry or you are straight and think that gay
people should be able to marry.

Employers are going to have to come down on one side of this issue or another if only because a long, drawn-out, and divisive debate
is not going to serve the productivity of the organization or individuals therein. It is very important that employers insist that the federal
court system rule on the constitutionality of DOMA laws for the same
reason it was untenable when interracial marriage was legal in some
places but not in others.

Q: If we hire someone married in another state to a same-sex partner, what are our obligations as far as benefits available to spouses?

A: This question gets to the crux of how same-sex marriage will
immediately affect organizations—whether they have DPBs or not.
The reason is that if an employee of yours who is gay goes to a place,
gets a marriage license, and gets married, he or she will consider himself or herself legally married. And, as the employer, you'll be
expected to treat his or her spouse equitably and just like any other
married employee. If you are in a state with a prohibition against
same-sex marriage—and certainly if you live in the United States you
have to contend with the government's stand not to recognize these
marriages—then you will be obligated to adhere to local and federal
law. The difficult challenge that lies ahead of us all, of course, is that
there will be a significant period of time in which the laws in one state
or five states or twenty-nine states may differ from those in others,
and also differ from federal law relative to marital status concerns.
Now, every gay individual who gets married will have to decide how
she or he reports these benefits. If they are going to file as married individuals, they will most certainly insist that you treat them, their
benefits, and the tax ramifications of those benefits accordingly.

Technically, an individual's relationship to government relative to tax obligations is between the individual and the government. Therefore, I have taken to advising clients to honor the marital status of the employee as the employee asserts it, treat that worker and his or her spouse as legally married, and don't assess the current tax ramifications of DPBs as if they were not married. I also advise all organizations to keep a separate accounting of benefits and what the tax ramifications would have been if they were still considering themselves partners and not married spouses. The truth is, if employers refuse to acknowledge the marriage license of their employees, they will likely find themselves in a confrontational situation (maybe even a lawsuit). Your employees will pull you into this debate in a way that will directly involve you.

Q: If your state expressly refuses to recognize same-sex marriages, how can someone pull you into a lawsuit for refusing to recognize the union?

A: It comes down to a person who gets married believing that the U.S. Constitution absolutely provides that the license she or he gets in one state will be honored by all of the other United States. So, while the various states where you might operate are trying to sort out whether they will recognize these licenses, employers will be put in a position of being between employees who insist that they are married—and have the licenses to prove it!—and states that believe they are under no obligation to recognize these licenses. So, every employer, if it treats a person contrary to what that person believes her or his marital status to be, will leave itself open to have its stance challenged in a court of law.

Chapter 9

It's Academic

I'm not the only gay adult who, having survived adolescence, feels a definite obligation to do anything possible to make it easier to grow up gay, lesbian, bisexual, asexual, or transgender in this country. There are lots of us all over the United States who go out of our way to mentor gay kids; to participate in activities of our schools' Gay-Straight Alliances (GSAs), whether we have kids or not; or who, like me, focus our efforts on educating adults in order to make the world safer for gay kids.

I always charge for the work I do, but schools can always get me cheap. So, if you're an educator or a school administrator who thinks that my brand of education would be helpful to your staff or faculty, don't hesitate to contact me. If I can't help, I know many people in organizations who can and will.

This chapter is a new addition in this edition and is dedicated to every member of the Gay, Lesbian and Straight Education Network (GLSEN) and to every other teacher, student, or staff member in America's schools, from elementary school through the university level, or any other person in the private or public sector who has ever done a single thing to raise awareness about the difficulties of growing up gay in America or who has ever lifted a finger to help a kid out just because it was the right thing to do. There are lots of you out there; I applaud you all.*

In this chapter, I provide an overview of the following salient issues for this topic. I know there are many more things that I could

---

* GLSEN is covered in some depth in this chapter, but is also included in Appendix I along with other organizations doing work addressing sexual orientation and gender identity related to youth and/or public education.

have included. They could fill a book of their own, and indeed the bibliography in Appendix I mentions a few that have tried.

- Sex education in the public schools
- GLSEN for educators
- GLSEN for students
- GLSEN for GSAs
- The state of sexual orientation and gender-identity studies in the United States, spring 2005
- Three studies
    - *Education Policy: Issues Affecting Lesbian, Gay, Bisexual, and Transgender Youth,* by Cianciotto and Cahill, published by the National Gay and Lesbian Task Force Policy Institute, New York, 2003
    - *The 2003 National School Climate Survey,* by Joseph G. Kosciw, published by GLSEN, December 2003
    - *Campus Climate for Gay, Lesbian, Bisexual, and Transgender People: A National Perspective,* by Susan R. Rankin, published by the NGLTF Policy Institute, New York, 2003.*

Two facts drove me to include this chapter and the material I've chosen for it:

1. It is frequently reported that 30 percent of all young people between the ages of twelve and twenty-one who attempt or commit suicide do so because they are not heterosexual and they fear retribution from family and friends.[1]
2. In schools and school systems with no GSAs, 68.2 percent of LGBT students report feeling unsafe due to their sexual orientation and/or gender identity. In schools that do have such a support organization, the percentage who report feeling unsafe is about 40 percent.[2] This is better, no doubt, but it is still too high.

There is much work for us all to do.

---

*Proper reference is given to material used from all three reports later in this chapter where appropriate. However, both NGLTF Policy Institute reports can be read/printed in their entirety from <www.ngltf.org>, and the *School Climate Survey* is available at <www.glsen.org>.

SEX EDUCATION IN THE PUBLIC SCHOOLS

A good place to begin doing the necessary work in order to have effective outreach to our young people, regardless of sexual orientation, about things related to human sexuality is in the schools, in sex-education programs.

I believe in encouraging abstinence from sex until people are old enough to emotionally and physically handle the responsibilities of intimacy in all its forms, but I'm also a practical woman. Adolescents experiment with sex and just about everything else, and although I might prefer that they stop losing their virginity at age thirteen or having kids before they're twenty, it's unlikely that such experimentation is going to stop. I'm frankly amazed at the unyielding, abstinence-only crowd: have they completely forgotten what it's like to be a teenager?

In the face of reality, then, informing our young people about the consequences of their actions and the many variations of human sexuality is the most important—no, it's the only—thing to do. They say it takes a village to raise a child? I agree with that sentiment, but it's in the matter of sex education that the village idiots are ever so likely to make their appearance.

For instance, the village idiots in my previous home state, Colorado, which is one of four states that do not mandate sex education, have seen to it that most kids don't get anything resembling sex education until they are seniors aged seventeen or eighteen. To say that it's too late at that point is a huge understatement. Colorado law also requires school districts to allow kids to opt out of any sex education course.

If you think it's hard for any teenager to reach out to adults to get information about staying safe and healthy, how do you think it is for gay teenagers? Again, in Colorado in spring 2004, the village idiots reared their heads again in the form of State Representative Shawn Mitchell, Republican, of Broomfield, who sponsored a bill that would have made it mandatory that absolutely no discussion of sexual orientation take place in the classroom, that if anything other than heterosexuality was going to be discussed that parents had to be notified in advance so they could opt-out their kids, and that parents had to be notified of what would be taking place in a sex education course.

The good news is that Colorado rose up and beat back the first two versions of Mitchell's bill. The bad news is that there is still a State Rep. and all his idiot supporters and compatriots trying to get such legislation passed.

If I sound a little angry, it's only because I am. Rep. Mitchell and his ilk are dangerous, destructive people who pander to a point of view to get votes and stay in power. They reject (if they bother to study at all) data about sexual orientation or sexual orientation identity and when it is known to most people. For instance, the average male knows his sexual orientation by the time he is thirteen; for females, the average age of awareness of her orientation identity is seventeen. The only thing that Representative Mitchell and others like him did and do to youth is make those who are homosexual ashamed, alienated, and perhaps suicidal and all youth afraid to reach out to the adults in their lives and proactively seek help in figuring out the maze of human sexuality in adolescence.

Sex education must be comprehensive, it must be honest, and it must be offered everywhere in this country beginning no later than the seventh grade and continuing all the way through high school. It should present a balanced view of all matters related to sexual activity, including abstinence, birth control, transmission of STDs, and how sex leads to pregnancy, which seems to be something a scary number of our kids don't know. In addition, it must present a fair and accurate view of human sexual orientation and gender identity.

If it doesn't, we are going to see teen pregnancy start to spike again, the transmission of STDs increase, and more young people killing themselves because their parents and teachers were absent emotionally and intellectually from their lives. If you want kids to make informed decisions, give them information.

GLSEN: WHAT IT IS, WHAT IT DOES

The Gay, Lesbian and Straight Education Network was started by Kevin Jennings in 1994. Their Web site, which is extensive, is listed in Appendix I. Their mission, generally speaking, is to educate educators about how best to deal with human sexuality—with an emphasis on, but not limited to, sexual orientation—in our public schools from K-12. I'm going to provide an overview of their functions, but first I'd like to cite two reasons why their existence is necessary, both of them from the very local news:

On March 19, 2004, it was reported that the Westminster School District of Westminster, California, had refused to recognize a California state law banning discrimination against transsexuals, a decision that could cost it millions of dollars in state and federal funding. Three of five trustees on the school board said they oppose the state law because they are Christians. "I might take a lot of heat for it today, but the rewards are going to be great in heaven," said one of the three trustees.[3] It's Christians like these who are working overtime to give Christians a bad name. Let's see if we can find some positive news somewhere.

On January 21, 2004, it was announced that the Guilford County Board of Education in Greensboro, North Carolina, passed a new antidiscrimination policy to protect all of its students from harassment and discrimination on the basis of their sexual orientation or gender identity. "Whatever you think about homosexuality or heterosexuality is not the issue here, it's how you treat students," said Gary Palmer, vice president of Replacements, Ltd. and cochair of the local GLSEN chapter in Greensboro.[4] It's businessmen like Gary Palmer, who is not a father and not even a teacher, who are working overtime to give community and civic leaders a good name.

It's clear that the three school board trustees in Westminster live and work in an environment that could be best described as six square miles surrounded by reality. Their position is completely indefensible. They are entitled to their opinions, of that there is no doubt, and I would fight to defend their rights to them. However, when their closed-mindedness results in possible serious civil inequities for a whole class of people who don't even come up in the Bible, then that is inexcusable.* We are talking about real people here: real teachers, real kids.

We are also talking about the fact that Greensboro, North Carolina, has an involved and active GLSEN chapter and Westminster, California, doesn't.

---

* If you think there's disagreement regarding the Bible and sexual orientation and what is said, and not said, in it about the topic, you are right. There is, and it's complicated and lasting. For every "biblical position" someone can come up with, I could come up with a counter "biblical position." Transgenderism is not mentioned at all, and so for people to vote as they did based on their "religious beliefs" just takes that whole phenomenon to the next utterly ridiculous, unjustifiable, and inexplicable level. Clearly their lack of knowledge and/or the degree to which they have their heads in the sand regarding human sexuality is profound, as is their unforgivable prejudice.

Helping People Help Themselves

To me, this is what GLSEN really does. Through education strate-gies, it enables teachers and students to help themselves and therefore help others regarding issues of human sexuality, especially sexual orientation and gender identity. The enemy of ignorance is informa-tion, always information. Disseminating information is the function and goal—always—of education. Give most people good informa-tion and the time to process it, and they will learn. This is the founda-tion of the work that I do in adult education, and it is the same in the schools. People may be professional educators, well trained, dedi-cated, and good at teaching, but if they don't know a subject, they will not teach it. GLSEN provides the tools to teach.

GLSEN divides itself into three main categories of resources: for educators, for students, and for chapters. Each division of labor, if you will, has a forum and a library designed specifically for those people. Beyond those common elements, a recent visit to their Web site revealed the following resources for each segment of the GLSEN world:

> *For educators:* Lesson planning and curriculum tools, teacher training programs, and classroom tools. One specific tool was a "marriage curriculum guide"; another was an "anti-bul-lying toolkit." The teacher training programs in particular are offered all over the United States and are open to faculty and staff from all over a given school district. GLSEN has been able, in many districts where it has established a presence, to make these teacher training programs eligible for profes-sional development recognition, which, of course, affects sal-ary rankings in some places.
>
> *For students:* The GLSEN Web site offers tips for organizing GSAs and doing peer-to-peer training programs. It also offers guides, resources, and information about common, national events such as the GLSEN-sponsored "Day of Silence." Day of Silence is the largest-ever youth-led event dedicated to ending discrimination on the basis of sexual orientation in the schools. It's a boycott on talking, basically, by all who partic-ipate on a given day in the school year. You may think such things are silly, but the Day of Silence in 2003, the first one,

got a lot of people talking—which, of course, was entirely the point.

For chapters: The GLSEN Web site represents a repository for all the things going on in the public school world regarding human sexuality that GLSEN is involved in or members should know about. Beyond the forums, discussion chat rooms, and library, the chapter segment also offers detailed plans about the annual GLSEN National Conference, typically held in the summer.

The tools and techniques and cohesion for a progressive movement addressed toward incorporating meaningful sex education in the schools as provided by GLSEN are extraordinary and extraordinarily important. Anyone working in the public schools, and especially the far-too-many teachers who find themselves in the closet at school, should fully investigate GLSEN in their part of the United States.

GAY-STRAIGHT ALLIANCES

GSAs are the employee networks of the school world, and their existence is important for all the same reasons. Kids want and need to reach out to others and know that they are not alone. Kids need and want to be involved in activities that are important to them as members of their school communities, regardless of sexual orientation. Kids need and want a place and a way to express themselves, teach others things they've learned about these subjects, and discuss current events related to sexual orientation with others who are similarly willing to share and explore. These are the functions of GSAs, and they are vital.

To those who say that such groups are unnecessary, or that they should be outlawed because they are not related to the curriculum, I say take your heads out of the sand. First, if you don't have a meaningful sex-ed program in your district, then shame on you and you should work to establish one. If you do have such a program, then the work of GSAs are very much curriculum related—certainly as much as the chess club, I'd say.

Even if you don't have sex education in your school or district, sexuality, sexual orientation, and gender identity are characteristics of people—and people, kids, are the essence of the schools. Anyone who thinks otherwise is another example of the village idiot.

HIGHER EDUCATION

Beyond the public schools, there is a new drive toward meaningful inclusion of sexual orientation and gender identity that goes beyond junior-college inclusion in something called a human sexuality course. According to a piece from March 2004 in the *Chicago Tribune*,[5] the University of Chicago is among other institutions such as UC Berkeley, NYU, Yale, San Francisco State College, and the University of Illinois at Urbana-Champaign, among others, that is offering courses with titles such as Social History of American Sexual Subcultures. Gay history, sexuality, and contributions to literature and the arts (Walt Whitman must get re-outed every fall to another incoming class who wasn't told that about him in high school) are becoming major parts of curricula at major and minor colleges and universities.

Take that, village idiots, you guardians of darkness. It is becoming more apparent to the rest of the world that even beyond same-sex marriage or the popularity of fluff such as *Queer Eye for the Straight Guy,* debates about sexuality are increasing and important. According to Dawne Moon, director of LGBT studies at the University of California, "More students want to know about it and gay studies programs help people sort out what's going on around them."[6] What a concept: education as a means for people to sort out what's going on around them. It almost drives me to suggest that the school board trustees of Westminster, California, at least consider auditing a course consisting of material from this century.

What might those courses look like if they considered my suggestion? As an example, I researched the undergraduate program in gender and sexuality studies at NYU, part of the Center for the Study of Gender and Sexuality (CSGS), which describes itself as offering "a broad interdisciplinary investigation of gender and sexuality . . . in its core curriculum, and insistently extending the view beyond U.S. borders."

That last mention of "beyond U.S. borders" I think is really important. Americans have a habit of viewing everything through the American point of view. I don't think there's a better country on the planet, but I recently read that only about 6 percent of American adults have ever visited another country. This is pitiful in and of itself, and when it comes to sexual orientation and gender identity, I can see how it would be incredibly useful for American students to learn that many countries are either very far ahead of us, or far behind us, in their inclusion based on these characteristics.

The CSGS curriculum general description goes on to say,

> At its core, the undergraduate Program encourages students to question the meanings of "male" and "female," as well as of sexual norms, in both Western and non-Western societies. Courses seek to unravel the ways in which ideas about gender and sexuality shape social roles and identities, in addition to the ways in which race, class, and ethnicity function in the experience of gender and sexuality within a culture. Gender and Sexuality Studies challenges the privileging of some categories (i.e., male or heterosexual) over others, along with the social and political implications of such hierarchies. Our curriculum makes gender and sexuality central rather than peripheral terms of analysis and seeks to complicate what is often presented as "natural" or "normal" in traditional academic curricula.[7]

Now, my dad is going to read that description and make note to my mom that they didn't have any of that stuff when he went to NYU (and then they're going to call me and remind me that he went to Columbia, but I'm trying to make a point here, folks). NYU or Columbia or whatever, he'll be right; they didn't. There are many things of significance in this program description: that they are breaking down male and female into their legitimate parts; that they are viewing the subjects through various filters as determined by various societal norms; that they are positioning orientation and gender identity with race and ethnicity so as to imply, or perhaps flat-out state, a recognition that these are inherent parts of the human condition. That they seek to "complicate what is often presented as normal or natural" gives me hope that the generations studying at NYU and other schools today are going to break through the barriers consistently thrown up by those who insist that homosexuality is unnatural and immoral. Of all the things I hope I live to see (such as when they release the report of who really shot JFK, or who Deep Throat was), I hope I live to see that breakthrough. That would be sweet.

If any of this whets your appetite as it does mine, then you may, as I was, be interested in what some of the actual courses in this curriculum are:

- Studying Gender, Studying Sexuality
- Sex, Gender, and the Bible
- Sex and Gender
- Gender in Early Christianity
- Sex, Gender, and Language
- Gay and Lesbian Performance
- Queer Cultures
- The Family
- Women and the Media
- Jewish Women in the Modern World
- Topics in Gender and Sexuality: Queer Families
- Topics in Gender and Sexuality: The Gender of War and Peace

I'm almost tempted to see if I can audit any of these classes online. Not only didn't they have these when my dad was a graduate student, they didn't have them twenty years ago when I was, either. All the better for students today and the world tomorrow that they have them now.

WHY IT ALL MATTERS

I hope if I have cause and opportunity to do another edition of this book that things such as DPBs and same-sex marriage will have greater clarity in our collective consciousness and so will require less space in the book. I would use that space for a more in-depth discussion of challenges and progress related to inclusion of sexual orientation and gender identity for our nation's and (since we are such a wonderful and influential country) the world's youth. For now, I would like to close by citing content and data from three very important reports that anyone who has kids or who works with kids or who knows kids (right, everyone) should be familiar with:

Education Policy: Issues Affecting Lesbian, Gay, Bisexual, and Transgender Youth

I chose to start here because of the table of contents of this report.[8] Just a listing of what they include should give you, my reader, a sense of all that is, could be, and must be involved:

1. LGBT Youth: A critical population
   a. Gay teen forced to read aloud from Bible at school: A profile of Thomas McLaughlin
   b. Methodological barriers to research on LGBT youth
   c. How many LGBT youth are there?
   d. Transgender youth
   e. Intersex youth
   f. Gender nonconformity: Making the connection—Judge rules that school must allow transgender youth to express her gender identity: Profile of Pat Doe
   g. LGBT youth of color: The "tricultural" experience
   h. Children of LGBT parents
   i. LGBT youth in foster care
   j. Homeless LGBT youth
   k. LGBT youth and their families
   l. Strength and resiliency of LGBT youth—More than just the "gay football captain": Profile of Corey Johnson
2. A grave picture of harassment and violence in schools
   a. Anti-LGBT harassment and violence in elementary and middle schools
   b. Anti-LGBT harassment and violence in high schools
   c. Sexual harassment in the public schools
   d. The impacts of anti-LGBT harassment and violence in all schools
3. Existing policy interventions
   a. The U.S. Constitution
   b. Federal Title IX and the Equal Access Act
   c. State policies
   d. Parental notification and "no promo homo" laws
   e. Staff development and training
   f. Curricula
   g. Safe-schools programs

   h. GSAs
   i. The Harvey Milk High School
4. Leaving our children behind: The No Child Left Behind Act
   of 2001
   a. Vouchers and school choice
   b. Charter schools
   c. Single-sex education
   d. Standardized testing
   e. Internet filtering
   f. LGBT youth and the Internet
   g. Violence prevention and unsafe schools
5. Abstinence-only until marriage sex education
   a. History
   b. Fear, Shame, and Misinformation
   c. Impact on HIV prevention
   d. Inherent sexism and antigay bias
   e. Sex ed and HIV prevention

In addition, there are the research standards and methods and a half-dozen appendixes. As you can see, there is a lot to cover, a lot to know. The thing is, in those places where they demand parental notification of the content of sex-ed classes, are they going to be this comprehensive on this part of human sexuality, forgetting for a moment (as if we can) the other vital elements of sex ed we must offer to keep our kids safe? Or are parents throughout the land going to continue to listen to the village idiots? I'm not a parent. If you are, I'd say you need to know not only what your kids are being taught—but what they are not being taught.

The 2003 National School Climate Survey

Key findings of this survey:[9]

- Unchecked harassment correlates with poor performance and diminished aspirations. LGBT youth who report significant verbal harassment are twice as likely to report they don't intend to go to college and their GPAs are significantly lower (2.9 versus 3.3).
- Supportive teachers can make a difference: 24.1 percent of LGBT students who cannot identify supportive faculty report

they have no intention of going to college. That figure is 10 percent when they can identify supportive faculty.
- Policymakers have an opportunity to improve school climates: LGBT students who did not have (or didn't know of) a policy protecting them from violence and harassment were nearly 40 percent more likely to cut school because they were afraid to go.*
- Harassment continues at totally unacceptable levels and is too often ignored: 84 percent of LGBT students report being verbally harassed because of their sexual orientation; 82.9 percent of these students report that faculty never or rarely intervene when present.†

Recommendations of the survey:

- Institute policies that include "sexual orientation and gender identity" as protected classes along with existing categories of race, religion, and ability.
- Provide training for teachers on how to support LGBT students.
- Create and support GSAs.

So now some of you are thinking that since GLSEN did the research and produced the report, of course they would recommend actions that are part of their overall mission statement. Well sometimes, just because a person or a group has an agenda doesn't mean that they are also not right on. Besides, the data clearly indicate not only a need for their existence but also for continued vigilance in adapting these strategies.

Campus Climate for GLBT People: A National Perspective

This study was conducted between October 2000 and December 2001.[10] It surveyed 1,000 students, 150 faculty, and 467 staff/administrators from fourteen institutions of higher learning all over the

---

* Forty-one states as of December 2003 *did not* have statewide policies to protect kids on the basis of sexual orientation and/or gender identity.
† Of all of the data (except for teen suicides) tied to orientation or identity, this is the most disturbing to me. What kind of a person stands there and lets a kid get bullied? They are either unarmed with appropriate information or strategies to deal with it or they are spineless. Either way, this is just terrible and must be corrected.

United States. Of these, 66 people had disabilities, 572 were gay (mostly male), 458 lesbian, 334 bisexual, 68 transgender, 848 women, 720 men, and 825 self-described as "closeted" in their environments.

A sampling of the findings follows (this is a 200-page report):

- 36 percent of LGBT undergrad students experienced harassment within a year of the survey, as have 29 percent of all respondents.
- 89 percent said the harassment was verbal and that students were, 79 percent of the time, the source of the derogatory comments.
- 20 percent feared for their physical safety and 51 percent concealed their orientation to avoid intimidation.
- 71 percent felt that LGBT people were likely to be harassed on their campus.
- 43 percent ranked their overall campus climate as "homophobic."
- 10 percent would avoid being seen on parts of campus known for being gay friendly.
- 41 percent said their institution was not addressing issues relative to sexual orientation and/or gender identity.
- 42 percent felt that the curriculum was not representative of LGBT people.
- 44 percent felt that there was any campus leadership around issues for LGBT people.
- 64 percent said that their work site or classroom accepted them as LGBT people.

This report has an in-depth listing of recommendations, which I have included as Appendix IV to this book because of their breadth and depth. I didn't want to leave anything out.

In conclusion, I'll say it one last time: whether you have kids or not, whether your kids are gay or transgender or not, we all have a responsibility to the children of this nation to see that they grow up in a culture of acceptance and understanding. It does take a village to raise a child; it does take the collective voices of a village to maintain the standards of a nation. The standards of our nation are succinctly put: with liberty and justice for all. And all means all.

Appendix I

Resources

ONLINE RESOURCES

Business

<www.echelonmagazine.com>: A new magazine focused on people in all industries and all sorts of organizational life. Sponsoring organization of a new LGBT business consortium and also an annual business conference. See their site for details.

<www.gaybusiness.com>: An excellent, comprehensive site about all aspects of either being gay in the business world or interacting with the LGBT community from an organizational standpoint.

Comprehensive General Resources and Research

<www.equalityproject.org>: The Equality Project promotes and monitors corporate adherence to contemporary business standards on sexual orientation policy for gay and lesbian consumers, employees, and investors.

<www.hrc.org>: The Human Rights Campaign: the largest lobbying organization representing the interests of the LGBT community to the federal government. A wealth of information, links, bibliographies, studies, and research is accessible through their site in general classifications of Family, Workplace, Community, and Law.

<www.ngltf.org>: The main organization is a premier resource for grassroots activism for LGBT issues in the United States. They break their work into various categories and operate at state, city, and local levels. Their Policy Institute is a premier research organization whose library is as extensive as any in the United States or elsewhere.

<www.outandequal.org>: An organization dedicated to bringing educational and marketing resources to organizations in the public and private sectors. Produces one of the best conferences of this kind annually in the United States. See their Web site for details.

<www.sldn.org>: The Soldier's Legal Defense Network is the sole national legal aid and watchdog organization that assists servicemembers hurt by the Don't Ask, Don't Tell, Don't Pursue policy.

Family and the Schools

<www.glsen.org>: Gay, Lesbian and Straight Education Network. See Chapter 9 for a complete description.

<www.pflag.org>: PFLAG is a national nonprofit organization with a membership of more than 77,000 households and more than 425 affiliates worldwide. This vast grassroots network is developed, resourced, and serviced by the PFLAG national office, located in Washington, DC; the national Board of Directors; and the Regional Directors' Council. Parents, Families and Friends of Lesbians and Gays promotes the health and well-being of gay, lesbian, bisexual, and transgendered persons, their families, and friends through: support, to cope with an adverse society; education, to enlighten an ill-informed public; and advocacy, to end discrimination and to secure equal civil rights. PFLAG provides opportunity for dialogue about sexual orientation and gender identity, and acts to create a society that is healthy and respectful of human diversity.

Legal

<www.glad.org>: Gay & Lesbian Advocates & Defenders. Location, Boston, works all over the country. Has an extensive Web site and links to additional resources. The lead attorneys on the Massachusetts same-sex marriage case are GLAD attorneys.

<www.lambda.org>: Another great resource for legal information and advice relative to sexual orientation.

Marketing

<www.trilliuminvest.com>: Your guide to socially responsible investing and activism.

<www.witeckcombs.com>: Witeck-Combs is a professional partnership committed to helping its clients match their strategic communications objectives with their business goals. They offer a broad range of communications services and work in partnership with similar marketing and advertising agencies all over the United States with a specialty in LGBT among other, cross-cultural, demographics (such as Harris Interactive and Merge Media Group).

Transgender

<www.donnarose.com>: A new site being developed by the incomparable Donna Rose, author of *Wrapped in Blue* (see Selected Bibliography for publication information) and another indispensable guide and colleague for me in the study of gender identity and transition.

<www.gendersanity.com>: The premier site (in my opinion) for information for transgender people and organizations working with and helping transitioning and transgender employees.

<www.taw.org>: Transgender at Work. They cover a lot of everything and the site is a wonderful resource for transgender people and HR people alike.

Workplace Education: Sexual Orientation, Gender Identity, DPBs

<www.common-grnd.com>: Common Ground is an education/consulting firm specializing in education focused on sexual orientation in the workplace and on domestic partner benefits. They offer a full-range of consulting on these and all related workplace issues.

SELECTED BIBLIOGRAPHY

All of the sites I've listed contain extensive bibliographies, so I've decided not to try to offer an extensive one here. Depending on your need and interest, books and recorded materials are available to you, and I suggest that you search on all the previously mentioned sites. However, I do have some personal favorites and so I've listed them here:

Aarons, Leroy (1995). *Prayers for Bobby.* San Francisco: HarperSanFrancisco.

Bagemihl, Bruce (1998). *Biological Exuberance: Animal Homosexuality and Natural Diversity.* New York: St. Martin's Press.

Boykin, Keith (1998). *One More River to Cross: Black and Gay in America.* New York: Anchor Books.

Davis, Kenneth (1998). *Don't Know Much About: The Bible.* Eagle Brook, IL.

Duberman, Martin (1993). *Stonewall.* New York: Dutton.

Eskridge, William Jr. (1996). *The Case for Same-Sex Marriage: From Sexual Liberty to Civilized Commitment.* New York: Free Press.

Helminiak, Daniel (1994).*What the Bible Really Says About Homosexuality.* San Francisco: Alamo Square Press.

STRAIGHT TALK ABOUT GAYS IN THE WORKPLACE

Jennings, Kevin (Ed.) (1994). *One Teacher in Ten: Gay and Lesbian Educators Tell Their Stories.* Boston: Alyson.

Lukenbill, Grant (1999). *Smart Spending: The Gay and Lesbian Guide to Socially Responsible Shopping and Investing.* Boston: Alyson.

Lukenbill, Grant (1999). *Untold Millions: Secret Truths About Marketing to Gay and Lesbian Consumers.* Binghamton, NY: The Haworth Press, Inc.

Rose, Donna (2003). *Wrapped in Blue: A Journey of Discovery.* Round Rock, TX: Living Legacy Press.

Signorile, Michelangelo (1995). *Outing Yourself: How to Come Out As Lesbian or Gay to Your Family, Friends, and Coworkers.* New York: Random House.

Wald, Michael, S. (1999). *The Wald Report, Same-Sex Couples, Marriage, Families and Children.* Stanford Law.

Appendix II

Tips for Transitioning People

PLANNING FOR TRANSITION ON THE JOB

General Preparation

You should be in therapy for several months before coming out at work. This is important for establishing your credibility with your employer, as well as for preparing yourself.

Work with your therapist to determine the best timing for coming out. Make sure he/she is prepared to assist you by talking to a designated person at work, and give him/her written permission to do so.

Come out to family and close friends (except coworkers and anyone who is likely to inform your employer). It's best to get this over with so it doesn't distract you while you transition at work.

Build a solid support system consisting of your therapist, a support group, and/or supportive friends or family. It's important to have a place outside work where you can talk about issues that arise on the job.

Gain some experience living in your target role. This will enable you to appear in your new role at work with confidence and ease.

Personal Appearance

Hormones should usually be started before coming out at work, but not too far in advance. When changes in appearance become pronounced (such as breast growth in women or facial hair growth in men), coming out cannot be delayed. If electrolysis is necessary on

Reprinted from the Center for Gender Sanity. Available online at <www.gendersanity.com/plan.shtml>.

your face and other visible areas, it should be mostly completed before you begin working in your new role.

Practice personal grooming (hair style, nails, etc.) so you are comfortable with these procedures before transitioning at work.

Acquire a professional wardrobe appropriate for your workplace and your position, taking care to avoid clothing that is too revealing. Shopping with a friend can be very helpful.

Making gradual changes in your appearance may soften the blow when you come out at work, but if you go too far, damaging rumors may start to circulate about you.

Work Situation

Find out whether your company has a nondiscrimination policy that covers gender identity or expression. If there is a dress code, familiarize yourself with the requirements for men and for women.

Research local laws to determine whether you have any legal protections. A lawsuit should be considered only as a last resort, but knowing your rights (if any) allows you to negotiate from a more solid position.

Find out if there is a gay and lesbian employee support group and, if so, whether they are informed about transgender issues. You may want to join this group even if you are not gay, because they may be supportive if they understand your needs.

If union membership is available to you, be an active member. Find out who to approach for support during your transition. Before you come out to management, inform this person about transsexualism and transition, and let her/him know about your plans.

Evaluate your relationships with coworkers. Your transition is more apt to be successful if you get along well with others beforehand. Cultivate friendly (not intimate) relationships with your coworkers. If you are particularly close to certain coworkers, you may want to come out to them before telling your employer, but beware of starting rumors that could reach your boss before you are ready.

Evaluate your standing with the company. Especially during the months before you transition, work to make your job performance excellent and increase your value as an employee if possible.

Documentation

If you have not legally changed your name, gotten a new driver's license, and amended your Social Security card, find out how to do so. These should be changed before you begin working in your new role.

Obtain copies of your most recent performance review and other documents your company may have on file concerning you. These can be important if your evaluations take a dive after you come out.

Begin keeping a notebook in which you keep a record of every event at work related to your transition. Make a note of every conversation you have, what was said, who was there, the date and time. Also record instances of behavior that might be discriminatory. Keep this record at home. Include any memos or other written material related to your transition.

If you send or receive e-mail at work relevant to your transition, forward it to your home account. Otherwise these messages are not your property and you may not have access to them later. Voice mail received at work should be transferred to your personal recorder.

Informing Superiors

Decide who to contact first. This could be a company psychologist, human resources person, employee assistance staff, supervisor, or upper management, depending on the structure of your company and your relationships with these people. Remember that people in some of these positions are more bound by rules of confidentiality than others.

Bring your employer some written matter, including basic information about transsexualism, information for employers about transitioning on the job, and a list of resources (books, articles, experts, consultants).

If possible, obtain information about other companies similar to yours where people have transitioned successfully, and the names of human resources personnel or managers who would be willing to talk to someone in your company.

Anticipate problems that are likely to arise in your particular workplace with any of your duties, specific coworkers or clients, sharing of restrooms or showers, etc. Have in mind some solutions to these potential problems. This will show your employer that you are sensitive to the feelings of others and willing to work as a team member to resolve difficulties.

Create a tentative timeline for yourself. Keeping in mind that these dates will remain flexible, decide when you'd like to begin working in your new role, when any transfers or changes in your job should take place, when you may need time off for surgeries, etc.

Have some pictures taken of yourself in professional clothing, whatever that means for your workplace and position. This helps to reassure your employer that you won't show up inappropriately dressed.

Let your employer know how to contact your therapist. Employers rarely find this necessary, but knowing that you have a therapist and that you're willing for them to talk helps to reassure your employer.

Ask to be included in planning your transition. Express your willingness to compromise and to coordinate your actions with a timeline approved by your employer.

Informing Coworkers

Write a letter to your coworkers explaining what you are planning to do and why it is important to you, acknowledging that it may be difficult for them and expressing your eagerness to help things go smoothly. Have the content and timing of your letter approved by your employer.

Obtain an example of a memo used in another company written by management to inform coworkers about a transsexual's plans to transition on the job. Suggest to your superiors that they use a similar format and send their memo in conjunction with your letter to your coworkers.

If there is no one in your company who is knowledgeable about transition in the workplace, suggest that your company hire a consultant to assist with the process.

Suggest that your company provide sensitivity training for your coworkers, as well as counseling for individuals who have difficulty dealing with your transition. A professional trainer who is an expert in transsexual issues is the best choice for providing this training. You should not do it because your coworkers may not feel free to ask personal questions, and professional boundaries may be breached. Your therapist may not be the best choice because of ethical considerations and because it reinforces the idea that transsexualism is a mental illness.

Offer to answer your coworkers' questions if you are comfortable doing so, but don't talk about the details of transsexualism and transition unless you are certain that everyone who can hear you wants to.

Plan B

Good planning maximizes your chances for successful transition on the job, but even the best planning can be thwarted by a high-ranking detractor. Think about what you will do if you lose your job.

Update your resume. Perhaps you will even want to send it out and go to some interviews in your new role to boost your confidence.

If you have thought about changing careers, find out what it would actually take to do so. You may want to take classes, pursue certification, or put in some applications to evaluate the feasibility of this path.

Save some money so you won't be desperate if you lose your job. Know what measures you could take to liquidate assets or reduce your expenses if necessary. Know who you can count on in case of emergency.

Don't plan on suing your employer if you lose your job. In most cases, there are no legal protections for transgendered employees, and discrimination may be impossible to prove. Lawsuits can be very expensive, and even if you have the money, you may not want to spend it on lawyers.

Appendix III

Assessment Questions

As explained in Chapter 5, there's nothing illegal about asking questions based on one's sexual orientation because, as we've seen in previous chapters, sexual orientation is not covered under any current federal law or act, and in the fourteen states and various jurisdictions that do provide for it in aspects of workplace protection, the whole idea is to help avoid discriminatory treatment. People who object to doing assessments fearing some always-nebulous, never-specified illegality are confusing thinking around EEO policy— i.e., disparate treatment of an included class of people—with reality. Asking questions about sexual orientation and/or gender identity does not create disparate treatment of a legally defined and protected class because gay and transgender people are not classified as such. Again, asking about the work environment relative to one's orientation means you are asking everyone—straight, gay, bisexual, or asexual—what they think. If you don't ask people what they think, how are you going to find out?

Please note that these are just a sampling. More questions about different aspects of work/life experience are available for discussion should you choose to contact me.

The purpose of this survey is to identify issues, obstacles, and best practices affecting gay, lesbian, bisexual, and transgender (GLBT) associates regarding work environment, productivity, and feeling fully valued. The survey is completely anonymous and you may feel free not to answer any question. Please do not note your name anywhere on the survey.

1. What part of the business are you in?
2. What is your title (optional)?
3. How long have you been with the company?
4. How do you identify yourself?
   _____ GLBT
   _____ Non-GLBT

5. I feel my opinions are valued.

_____ Not at all

_____ Somewhat

_____ Haven't thought about it

_____ Very

_____ Completely

_____ Not applicable

6. I feel free to express my opinions.
7. I feel included in formal work groups.
8. I feel included in informal work groups.
9. I feel my sexual orientation affects the advancement of my career.
10. I am "out" at work.
11. I feel physically safe at work.
12. I feel comfortable sharing my personal life with unit members.
13. I feel comfortable supporting GLBT issues at work.
14. Senior leadership in my area is supportive of GLBT associates.
15. My office has effective diversity education efforts regarding GLBT issues.
16. My office's efforts have improved the work environment for GLBT associates.
17. I feel that this organization values the diversity that GLBT associates bring to it.
18. I would recommend working here to GLBT friends.

Answer the following questions "yes" or "no." If yes and you choose to elaborate, you may do so in the comments section below.

Within the past 24 months, I have been the target of inappropriate behavior or comments at work on the basis of perceived sexual orientation or gender identity. _____

Within the past 24 months, I have witnessed inappropriate behavior or comments directed at someone else based on their perceived sexual orientation or gender identity. _____

Of the following, the three statements that have or could have the most positive effect on productivity are:

_____ Being in an environment where people are supportive of each other

_____ Having nondiscrimination policies that include sexual orientation and/or gender identity

_____ Having opportunities for career advancement

_____ Being able to build coalitions with other workplace diversity groups

_____ Having organizational resources for employee groups

_____ Participating in an affinity group that contributes to the company's objectives

_____ Having diversity education that includes sexual orientation

_____ Having domestic partner benefits

_____ Having mentoring programs based on sexual orientation, race, gender, age, and/or disability

_____ Having mentoring programs not based on any of the above

Appendix IV

Campus Climate Survey
Recommendations

Recruit and Retain GLBT Individuals

- Provide services to potential employees to assist their same-sex partners in securing employment.
- Actively recruit and retain GLBT persons.
- Actively recruit and retain heterosexual students and staff supportive of GLBT equality.
- Include sexual orientation and gender identity or expression in the institution's nondiscrimination clause.
- Extend employee spousal benefits (health insurance, tuition remission, sick and bereavement leave, use of campus facilities, child care services, comparable retirement plans) to domestic partners.
- Provide single stall gender-neutral restroom facilities.
- Provide housing for same-sex partners.
- Develop visible scholarships targeting GLBT students.

Demonstrate Institutional Commitment to GLBT Issues/Concerns

- Integrate GLBT concerns into university documents/publications (grievance procedures, housing guidelines, application materials).
- Create a GLBT alumni group within the existing alumni organization.
- Create a documentation form in police services for reporting hate crimes committed against GLBT people.
- Create a standing advisory committee on GLBT issues similar to other university standing committees (e.g., on race and ethnicity, dis-

Reprinted from: Rankin, Susan R. (2003). *Campus Climate for Gay, Lesbian, Bisexual, and Transgender People: A National Perspective.* New York: The National Gay and Lesbian Task Force Policy Institute, p. 7. Available online at <www.ngltf.org>.

ability, etc.) that advise the administration on constituent group issues and concerns.
- Provide a clear, safe, visible means of reporting acts of intolerance.
- Include openly GLBT people on university committees.
- Respond visibly and expeditiously to acts of intolerance directed at GLBT members of the community.
- Provide a victim's advocate in the public safety office trained for the particular needs of GLBT people.
- Provide visible "safe" persons, within campus security, student life and other departments, for GLBT victims of harassment to alleviate fear of revictimization.

Integrate GLBT Issues/Concerns into Curriculum and Pedagogy

- Create a GLBT studies center or department.
- Provide release time to faculty for GLBT course development.
- Expand GLBT-related library holdings.
- Integrate GLBT issues into existing courses, where appropriate.
- Promote the use of inclusive language in the classroom (for example, create a pamphlet with examples of heterosexist assumptions and language with suggested alternatives).
- Produce or purchase audiovisual materials that can be used by all faculty to introduce GLBT materials.
- Provide course credit to GLBT students for peer education initiatives.

Provide Educational Programming on GLBT Issues/Concerns

- Include sexual orientation and gender identity issues in student orientation programs.
- Include sexual orientation and gender identity issues in new faculty/staff orientations.
- Develop workshops/programs to address GLBT issues within residence life, especially geared toward resident assistants.
- Develop workshops/programs to address homophobia/heterosexism within fraternities, sororities and intercollegiate athletics.
- Sponsor lectures, concerts, symposia, and other activities to increase GLBT awareness on campus.

- Provide training for campus health care professionals to increase their sensitivity to issues of sexual orientation and gender identity and the special health needs of GLBT individuals.
- Provide training sessions for public safety officers on GLBT issues and concerns and anti-GLBT violence.

Create Safe Spaces for Dialogue and Interaction

- Create an office for GLBT concerns.
- Create safe space for inter-/intra-group dialogue and discourse (book clubs, brown bags, etc.).
- Create GLBT groups for under-represented populations (GLBT people who are physically or mentally challenged, GLBT people of color, GLBT international people, transgender people, etc.).
- Create and identify a designated safe, social GLBT meeting place.

Appendix V

Strategies for Managing Transition

When confronted with an employee who plans to transition from one sex to the other, employers have reacted in a wide variety of ways, some of which have worked better than others. Where transition has been smoothest, the following strategies have been used.

- *Talk with the Transsexual Employee.* Find out when the employee would like to start working in the new role, whether she/he anticipates any problems with transitioning, and whether she/he would like any temporary or permanent changes in duties or responsibilities. The transsexual employee can also be a source of useful information about transsexualism, how transition has been handled in other workplaces, and who to contact for further information and training.
- *Assemble a Transition Team.* A team to oversee the transition process should include the transsexual person, his/her manager, and a human resources professional, at the very least. It may also include a union representative, other managers, and an outside consultant. Confidentiality is extremely important at this stage because leakage of information about the impending transition before strategies are in place to deal with it can lead to an unmanageable situation.
- *Educate the Team.* The transition team should educate itself regarding transsexualism and transition issues. Unless one or more people on the team have dealt with transition in a similar situation, outside experts and/or resource materials are needed to provide this training. The transsexual worker can be a valuable source for reading material and contacts but should not be expected to educate the team.
- *Determine Timing.* The main factor in the timing of the transition is the transsexual employee's readiness to start working in her/his new role. Some transsexual workers prefer to coordinate their transition with a vacation period to give themselves and their coworkers time to adjust. Coworkers should be informed shortly before the transsexual

employee is to change roles and should receive sensitivity training as soon as they are informed.

- *Inform Others.* People who work in direct contact with the transsexual employee on a daily basis, and perhaps others who have more limited contact, should be informed about the transition in advance. People may be informed by a written memo, by email, in a meeting, or some combination of these ways. Whatever the medium, management should provide a clear message expressing confidence in and support for the transsexual employee and the expectation that he/she will be treated with respect.

- *Provide Training.* Some employees have concerns about working with a transsexual person. In the absence of reliable information, they will turn to myths and misinformation or simply make up "facts," setting the stage for intolerance and hostility. Training should be provided by outside consultants or human resources professionals who are experts on transsexual issues. Be prepared to offer training earlier than planned if coworkers find out about the transsexual employee sooner than intended.

- *Model Desired Behavior.* Most people in the workplace have had little or no experience interacting with a transsexual person. The most powerful influence in determining how they will act are the examples that are set for them by supervisors, managers, and executives. People in positions of authority should be coached to model respectful behavior.

- *Change Documents.* The transsexual employee is responsible for obtaining a legal name change, new social security card, and new driver's license. At the time of transition, all employee records must be changed to reflect her/his new name and sex. New photographs will have to be taken for identificaiton badges. Discuss with the transsexual employee the best timing for changing her/his status on medical benefits plans.

- *Restroom Use.* The transsexual employee should begin using the restroom appropriate for his/her new gender role immediately upon transitioning. If coworker discomfort makes this arrangement difficult, a temporary compromise can be employed to give everyone time to get used to the new situation. Compromises can take many forms; consultation with an expert can help to find the best arrangement for your specific workplace needs. If locker rooms or showers are part of the workplace, plans will be needed for use of these facilities as well.

- *Assess Client Needs.* If the transsexual employee deals with vendors, clients, customers, or the public, decide how these contacts will be handled. Depending on the situation, clients may be informed before transition takes place, or management can prepare a statement and wait for clients to inquire.

- *Be Proactive.* In addition to deciding how to handle the issues on this list, the transition team should anticipate other problems that might arise in your speicific setting with the particular people involved. Each workplace is unique and can present its own set of challenges. The team should develop solutions to any anticipated problems, using outside consultants and resource materials when necessary.
- *Prevent Hostility.* Hostility can arise in a transsexual employee's coworkers when they don't understand transsexualism, when they think the transsexual person is being given preferential treatment, and when diversity is not appreciated in the work environment. The likelihood of hostile reactions can be reduced by establishing a culture of appreciation of differences, providing adequate training, and treating all employees fairly.
- *Monitor Adjustment.* Transsexual employees may not report harassment because they don't want to cause trouble or because they fear repercussions from their coworkers or supervisors. A management or human resources representative should take the initiative in ongoing assessment of employee adjustment to transition.
- *Provide Counseling.* Counseling should be provided for employees who have ongoing difficulty working with a transsexual person. Employee assistance programs, counseling staff, or outside therapists can provide this service. Employees should be reminded of the availability of this resource.
- *Deal with Complaints.* Any complaints of harassment or discrimination should be investigated and dealt with promptly, whether they are directed against the transsexual worker or other employees. Procedures already in place to deal with other types of unacceptable behavior can be used.

Notes

Chapter 1

1. Witeck-Combs/Harris Interactive, "6 of 10 heterosexuals say benefits for married heterosexual employees should be equally available for employees in same-sex couples," Second Annual Survey, October 2003. Available online at <www.witeckcombs.com>.

2. "Brain differences seen in gay sheep," Reuters, March 9, 2004. Available online at <www.abc.net.au/news/newitems/s1061683.htm>.

3. Bruce Bagemihl, *Biological exuberance: Animal homosexuality and natural diversity* (New York: St. Martin's Press, 1998).

4. Alfred Kinsey, Wardell B. Pomeroy, and Clyde E. Martin, *Sexual behavior in the human male* (Philadelphia: W.B. Saunders, 1948); Alfred Kinsey, Wardell B. Pomeroy, Clyde E. Martin, and Paul Gebhard, *Sexual behavior in the human female* (Philadelphia: W.B. Saunders, 1953).

5. Dean Hamer, *The science of desire: The search for the gay gene and the biology and behavior* (New York: Simon & Schuster, 1994); Simon LeVay, *The sexual brain* (Cambridge, MA: MIT Press, 1993).

6. Witeck-Combs/Harris Interactive, "HRC public report," February 2004. Available online at <www.witeckcombs.com>.

7. Ibid.

8. Human Rights Campaign, "Gay families deserve nothing less than equality under the law," January 22, 2004. Available online at <www.hrc.org>.

9. Frank Newport, "Iraq, economy remain most important problems," Gallup News Service, Gallup Polls, December 13, 2004. Available online at <www.gallup.com/polls>.

10. Witeck-Combs/Harris Interactive, "6 of 10 heterosexuals say," 2003.

11. Human Rights Campaign, "Workplace." Available online at <www.hrc.org/workplace>.

12. Harris Interactive/Witeck-Combs, "New Harris Interactive/Witeck-Combs Internet survey confirms gays and lesbians are among heaviest Internet users," April 2000. Available online at <www.witeckcombs.com>.

13. Statistics available online from the Gill Foundation at <www.gillfoundation.com>.

14. Witeck-Combs/Harris Interactive, "HRC public report," 2004.

15. Richard Florida, "Gay-tolerant societies prosper economically," *USA Today,* May 1, 2003, p. 13A.

Chapter 2

1. Journal Register News Service, available online at <www.journalregister. com>.

2. Louise Young, *State of the workplace report* (Washington, DC: The Human Rights Campaign, 1999). Available online at <www.hrc.org>.

3. Witeck-Combs/Harris Interactive, "HRC public report," February 2004. Available online at <www.witeckcombs.com>.

4. Witeck-Combs/Harris Interactive, "6 of 10 heterosexuals say benefits for married heterosexual employees should be equally available for employees in same-sex couples," Second Annual Survey, October 2003. Available online at <www. witeckcombs.com>.

5. Ibid.

6. Alistair D. Williamson, "Is this time right to come out?" *Harvard Business Review,* July 1, 1993, p. 43.

7. Ibid.

8. Ibid.

9. Paul Johnson, "LGBT federal workers lose job protections," *365gay.com,* March 17, 2004. Available online at <www.365gay.com>.

10. Parents, Families and Friends of Lesbians and Gays, available online at <www.pflag.org>.

Chapter 3

1. Cooper Thompson, "Visions" (Cambridge, MA: The Campaign to End Homophobia, 1990).

2. Gregory Herek, "Heterosexuals' attitudes toward lesbians and gay men: Correlates and gender differences," *The Journal of Sex Research,* November 1998, pp. 45-48.

3. Kaiser Family Foundation Polls and Studies, "Sexual orientation in the workplace." Available online at <www.kff.org>.

4. "Just the facts about sexual orientation and youth: A primer for principals, educators, and school personnel," a collaborative publication by the American Academy of Pediatricians, American Counseling Association, American Association of School Administrators, American Federation of Teachers, American Psychological Association, American School Health Association, Interfaith Alliance Foundation, National Association of School Psychologists, National Association of Social Workers, and National Education Association, 1999. Available online at <www. apa.org>.

5. Paul Gebhard, *Sex offenders: An analysis of types* (New York: Harper & Row, 1985).

6. Ibid.

Chapter 4

1. Stanley Coren, *The left-hander syndrome: The causes and consequences of left-handedness* (New York: Free Press, 1992).
2. New York Business Group on Health, "Report on HIV/AIDS education for adults in the workplace," 1990.
3. Sara Rynes and Benson Rosen, "Profiting from others' experience: A diversity training checklist," *HR Magazine,* October 1994, pp. 22-23, 66-67.
4. Daniel Helminiak, *What the Bible really says about homosexuality* (San Francisco: Alamo Square Press, 1994).
5. Bruce Bagemihl, *Biological exuberance: Animal homosexuality and natural diversity* (New York: St. Martin's Press, 1998).
6. Alfred Kinsey, Wardell B. Pomeroy, and Clyde E. Martin, *Sexual behavior in the human male* (Philadelphia: W.B. Saunders, 1948); Alfred Kinsey, Wardell B. Pomeroy, Clyde E. Martin, and Paul Gebhard, *Sexual behavior in the human female* (Philadelphia: W.B. Saunders, 1953).
7. Lisa Bennett, *Mixed blessings: Mainstream religion and gay and lesbian Americans* (Washington, DC: The HRC Foundation, 1999). Available online at <www.hrc.org>.

Chapter 5

1. Janis Walworth, "Employers guide to transgender employees," Center for Gender Sanity. Available online at <www.gendersanity.com>.
2. Lynn Conway, "How frequently does transsexualism occur?" 2002. Available online at <www.ai.eecs.umich.edu/people/conway/TS/TSprevalence.html>.
3. Janis Walworth and Liz Winfeld, "Transgender issues in the workplace," in *A trainer's guide to training tough topics* (New York: American Management Association, 2001).
4. Janis Walworth, "Managing transsexual transition in the workplace," Center for Gender Sanity, 2003, p. 2. Available online at <www.gendersanity.com>.
5. Harry Benjamin International Gender Dysphoria Association, "The standards of care for gender identity disorders, Version six," 2001. Available online at <www.hbigda.org>.
6. Walworth, "Managing transsexual transition," 2003.

Chapter 6

1. Kathleen Taney, "Vend supplier diversity: Big changes at Big Blue; IMB introduces America's first GLBT vendor program," *Echelon,* March/April 2004. Available online at <www.echelonmagazine.com>.
2. Juan Battle, Cathy Cohen, Dorian Warren, Gerard Fergerson, and Suzette Audam, "Say it loud: I'm black and I'm proud; Black pride survey 2000." Available online at <www.thetaskforce.org>.
3. Louise Young, *State of the workplace report* (Washington, DC: The Human Rights Campaign, 1999). Available online at <www.hrc.org>.

Chapter 7

1. Edward E. Hubbard, *Measuring diversity results,* Volume 1 (Petaluma, CA: Global Insights Publishing, 1997).

2. "'Intolerant tag' deters businesses from Utah," *The Denver Post,* March 22, 2004, Business section, p. 3.

3. The Deluxe Corporation and Deluxe Corporation Advisory Council, "The business case for diversity," [internal brochure] 1998.

4. Shell Exploration and Production Company, "Diversity Performance Standard, created by a cross-functional team from various business units' Diversity Action Teams," 1999.

5. Ibid.

6. Ibid. (italics added for emphasis).

7. Overlooked Opinions Inc., "Mulryan/Nash–Simmons Market Research Report—Sexual orientation and the market," 1998.

8. Witeck-Combs/Harris Interactive, "The gay and lesbian market: New trends, new opportunities," 2004. Available online at <www.witeckcombs.com>.

9. These figures are from the Selig Center for Economic Growth at the University of Georgia.

10. "Queer life at Yale: A guide for students," Larry Kramer Initiative Fund for Lesbian and Gay Studies at Yale, 2003. Available online at <www.yale.edu/lesbiangay/homepage.html>.

11. Overlooked Opinions Inc., "Mulryan/Nash–Simmons Market Research Report," 1998.

12. Unless otherwise noted, all research bulleted here comes from Witeck-Combs/Harris Interactive between 2001 and March 2004. Available online at <www.witeckcombs.com>.

13. Witeck-Combs/Harris Interactive, "Why market to the gay community: Answers to the top ten questions asked by smart marketers," November 2002. Available online at <www.witeckcombs.com>.

14. Ibid.

15. Valerie Seckler, "Targeting gays: Affluent market largely ignored," March 2004. Available online at <www.gsb.sanford.edu/pdf>.

16. Witeck-Combs/Harris Interactive, "Why market to the gay community," 2002.

17. Ibid.

18. Michael Wilke, "Volvo bids for gay families," The Commercial Closet. Available online at <www.planetout.com>.

19. Ibid.

20. Daniella Aird, "Builders tailor homes, marketing to interest gay buyers," *South Florida Sun-Sentinel* (Broward Metro Edition, Fort Lauderdale), March 8, 2001, p. 1A.

21. Commercial Closet Association, "Mainstream B2B advertising best practices." Available online at <www.commercialcloset.com>.

22. Kathleen Taney, "Vend supplier diversity: Big changes at Big Blue; IBM introduces America's first GLBT vendor program," *Echelon,* March/April 2004. Available online at <www.echelonmagazine.com>.

23. The Equality Project, "The equality principles." Available online at <www.equalityproject.org>.

24. Human Rights Campaign, "Corporate equality index on gay, lesbian, bisexual, and transgender social responsibility" (Washington, DC: Human Rights Campaign, 2004). Available online at <www.hrc.org>.

25. Michael Markowitz, "Shareholders' power is the new weapon in fight for equality," *Newsday,* January 4, 2004.

Chapter 8

1. Marc A. Rogers (Part one) and Daley Dunham (Part two), *Contracts with equality: An evaluation of the San Francisco Equal Benefits Ordinance* (Amherst, MA: The Institute of Gay and Lesbian Strategic Studies, 2003). Available online at <www.iglss.org>.

2. Society of Human Resources Management, "Human resources management issues and trends" (June 16) (Alexandria, VA: Society of Human Resources Management, 1999).

3. The Employee Benefits Research Group, "Effective employee benefits" (Washington, DC: Employee Benefits Research Group, 1992). Available online at <www.ebrg.org>.

4. Human Rights Campaign, "Clear plurality of Americans favor same-sex marriage and civil unions." Available online at <www.hrc.org>.

5. *The Denver Post,* February 22, 2004, Business section brief, p. 2. As picked up from the AP.

Chapter 9

1. Jason Cianciotto and Sean Cahill, "Education policy: Issues affecting lesbian, gay, bisexual, and transgender youth" (Washington, DC: National Gay and Lesbian Task Force Policy Institute, 2003). Available online at <www.ngltf.org>.

2. GLSEN, "Release of 2003 National School Climate Survey sheds new light on the experiences of LGBT students in America's schools." Available online at <www.glsen.org>.

3. *The Denver Post,* March 19, 2004, p. 23.

4. "Anti-bias policy by board hailed as courageous." *News and Record,* Greensboro, NC, January 21, 2004, p. A1.

5. Ken Denning, "Gay studies flourish in academia as topic grains urgency." *Chicago Tribune,* March 2004.

6. Ibid.

7. Quote taken from the Center for the Study of Gender and Sexuality (CSGS) curriculum description, available online at <www.nyu.edu>.

8. Cianciotto and Cahill, "Education Policy," 2003.

9. Joseph G. Kosciw, *The 2003 National School Climate Survey: The school-related experiences of our nation's lesbian, gay, bisexual, and transgender youth* (New York: The Gay, Lesbian, and Straight Education Alliance Network, 2004). Available online at <www.glsen.org>.

10. Susan R. Rankin, "Campus climate for gay, lesbian, bisexual, and transgender people: A national perspective" (New York: NGLTF Policy Institute, 2003). Available online at <www. ngltf.org>.

Index

Order a copy of this book with this form or online at:
http://www.haworthpress.com/store/product.asp?sku=5403

STRAIGHT TALK ABOUT GAYS IN THE WORKPLACE
Creating an Inclusive, Productive Environment for Everyone in Your Organization, Third Edition

_____in hardbound at $39.95 (ISBN: 1-56023-546-2)

_____in softbound at $19.95 (ISBN: 1-56023-547-0)

Or order online and use special offer code HEC25 in the shopping cart.

COST OF BOOKS_____

POSTAGE & HANDLING_____
*(US: $4.00 for first book & $1.50
for each additional book)*
*(Outside US: $5.00 for first book
& $2.00 for each additional book)*

SUBTOTAL_____

IN CANADA: ADD 7% GST_____

STATE TAX_____
*(NJ, NY, OH, MN, CA, IL, IN, PA, & SD
residents, add appropriate local sales tax)*

FINAL TOTAL_____
*(If paying in Canadian funds,
convert using the current
exchange rate, UNESCO
coupons welcome)*

☐ **BILL ME LATER:** (Bill-me option is good on
US/Canada/Mexico orders only; not good to
jobbers, wholesalers, or subscription agencies.)
☐ Check here if billing address is different from
shipping address and attach purchase order and
billing address information.

Signature_____

☐ **PAYMENT ENCLOSED: $_____**

☐ **PLEASE CHARGE TO MY CREDIT CARD.**

☐ Visa ☐ MasterCard ☐ AmEx ☐ Discover
☐ Diner's Club ☐ Eurocard ☐ JCB

Account # _____

Exp. Date_____

Signature_____

Prices in US dollars and subject to change without notice.

NAME_____

INSTITUTION_____

ADDRESS_____

CITY_____

STATE/ZIP_____

COUNTRY_____ COUNTY (NY residents only)_____

TEL_____ FAX_____

E-MAIL_____

May we use your e-mail address for confirmations and other types of information? ☐ Yes ☐ No
We appreciate receiving your e-mail address and fax number. Haworth would like to e-mail or fax special
discount offers to you, as a preferred customer. **We will never share, rent, or exchange your e-mail address
or fax number.** We regard such actions as an invasion of your privacy.

Order From Your Local Bookstore or Directly From

The Haworth Press, Inc.

10 Alice Street, Binghamton, New York 13904-1580 • USA
TELEPHONE: 1-800-HAWORTH (1-800-429-6784) / Outside US/Canada: (607) 722-5857
FAX: 1-800-895-0582 / Outside US/Canada: (607) 771-0012
E-mail to: orders@haworthpress.com

For orders outside US and Canada, you may wish to order through your local
sales representative, distributor, or bookseller.
For information, see http://haworthpress.com/distributors

(Discounts are available for individual orders in US and Canada only, not booksellers/distributors.)

PLEASE PHOTOCOPY THIS FORM FOR YOUR PERSONAL USE.
http://www.HaworthPress.com

BOF04

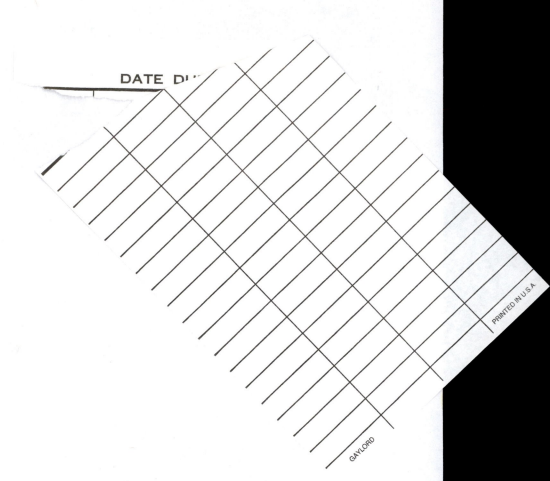